GUNPOWDER GIRLS

GUNPOWDER GIRLS

THE TRUE STORIES OF THREE CIVIL WAR TRAGEDIES

TANYA ANDERSON

QUINDARO

Quindaro Press • Kansas City, Missouri

Publisher's Cataloging-In-Publication Data
(Prepared by The Donohue Group, Inc.)

Names: Anderson, Tanya.
Title: Gunpowder girls : the true stories of three Civil War tragedies / by Tanya Anderson.
Description: Kansas City, Missouri : Quindaro Press, 2016. | Interest age level: 14 and up. | Includes bibliographical references and index.
Identifiers: LCCN 2016940762 | ISBN 978-0-9669258-7-6
Subjects: LCSH: Gunpowder industry--Accidents--United States--History--19th century. | Women--Employment--United States--History--19th century. | Ammunition--United States--History--19th century. | United States--History--Civil War, 1861-1865--War work. | United States--History--Civil War, 1861-1865--Women.
Classification: LCC HD9663.U62 A54 2016 | DDC 338.4/7623450973--dc23

Published by Quindaro Press
3808 Genessee Street
Kansas City, Missouri 64111
www.quindaropress.com

2 4 6 8 10 9 7 5 3 1

To my mother, Pat Zimmers, and to all of the women who work or have worked to make sure their children had food to eat, clothes to wear, and a roof over their heads.

CONTENTS

PART III:

Stars and Fire at the Washington Arsenal
Washington, D.C. • June 17, 1864

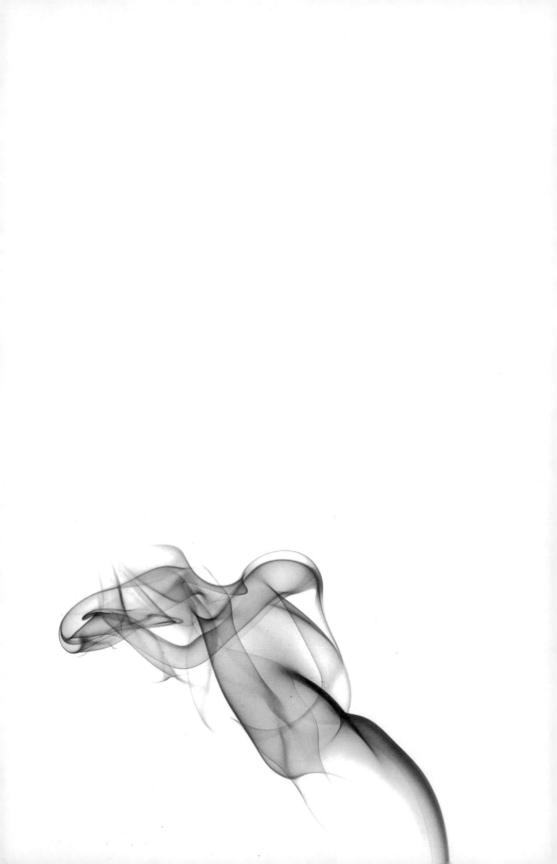

INTRODUCTION

WOMEN AND WAR. One brings life into the world and the other takes life away. Throughout history, women have been the healers, the supporters, and the strong foundations for families and friendships. They have championed causes that lift up those who have been pushed down by society and government. When they could not lead through power, women have led by example. In early American history, the familiar names of Ann Bradstreet, Abigail Adams, Dolley Madison, Sacajawea, and Lucretia Mott have not faded from our national story. Their lives remind us of the intelligence, strength, and sacrifices women have offered and the difference they have made in growing our country.

The mismatch of calico hoop skirts in rooms filled with gunpowder and bullets illustrates a time when old rules and roles had to change. The Civil War brought not only change, but also unexpected levels of suffering to soldiers and civilians alike. Mothers, wives, sisters, and daughters had to find a way to survive while their men were away fighting, because there was no man at home to earn a living. (Some, but not all, soldiers did send home money, but it was not enough and was often delayed for months.) Some families lost all of their sons in battle. Nearly 620,000 soldiers died, and another 500,000 were seriously injured, many disabled for life. This remains the highest number of military deaths our nation has ever experienced. The suffering did not end with the war.

But somewhere in all the information that has been written about the Civil War—its battles, its soldiers, and its causes—we find precious little about the other half of the American population: the women.

Women got involved in wartime work and moved from their old roles into new ones. They put their hearts and hands to work to fill the gaps left when their men enlisted. While some hands knitted socks and gloves (or mittens, as the pacifist Quaker women did—to eliminate a "trigger finger"), other women's hands held onto the wooden handles of a horse-drawn plow. Hands that had never known a callus were chopping wood, planting seeds, and holding the reins of a horse. These hands may have been smaller than a man's, but they were just as able to work a farm as they were to comfort a sick child.

Immigrant girls brought what skills their hands could produce and used them to earn a living in the U.S. They worked long hours cleaning houses that were not theirs and making clothes they would never wear in order to earn just enough to support themselves and their families.

More than two dozen arsenals were in operation to supply both the Union and Confederate armies with guns and ammunition. By the middle of the first year of the war, these working-class women and girls—some of whom were mere children—had taken jobs in these arsenals. Their small, feminine hands touched materials they had never handled before, putting gunpowder and lead into small paper cartridges. They put their lives in the hands of the governments that employed them.

These three stories are theirs.

Part I

CATASTROPHE
at the Allegheny Arsenal

**LAWRENCEVILLE,
PENNSYLVANIA
SEPTEMBER 17, 1862**

My sister and I walked to work from our home at Penn Avenue and Seventeenth Street that morning as usual. It was payday. The morning passed quickly. We did not stop for lunch at 12 o'clock on account of the rush. [...]

At 2 o'clock another girl and I were the only persons in Room 13. Suddenly there was a terrific roar; the earth seemed to split apart. The girl with me jumped through a window and I followed her, alighting on top of her in some grass behind the building. I lifted her to her feet and we started to run towards Butler Street. As we ran, there was a second explosion, and before we reached the street a third one.

Looking around we saw the building we had just left being torn to pieces. My sister escaped in some manner. She has never been able to tell just how. I was a nervous wreck for several weeks, and so terribly shocked that night that I had to be held in bed by force.[1]

—Mary McCandless McGraw, who was 13 years old when the Allegheny Arsenal explosion occurred

Chapter One

ALL IN A DAY'S WORK AT THE ARSENAL

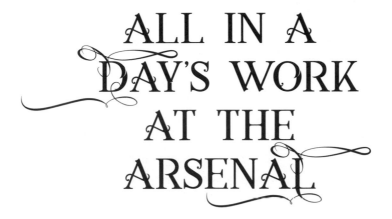

THE SUMMER'S HEAT AND HUMIDITY LINGERED IN THE DAWNING HOURS OF WEDNESDAY, SEPTEMBER 17, 1862. Dozens of women and girls of Lawrenceville, Pennsylvania, a suburb of Pittsburgh, tied on their bonnets, picked up their dinner bundles, and set out for another day of work at the nearby Allegheny Arsenal. (What people called "dinner" back then, we would call "lunch" today.) They looked forward to picking up their monthly pay during their midday break, but that was still six or seven hours away.

Some of the girls lived close to the arsenal, but not as close as the officers and the other men who worked there. The men lived in the barracks on 39th Street, a part of the arsenal complex, which stretched from the Allegheny River to the north to Penn Avenue on the south. Most of the female workers had a long trek each day—twenty blocks or more—leaving before dawn and returning home after dark, especially during the winter when hours of daylight are short.

As they encountered coworkers along the way, the girls made small talk, many with a strong Irish brogue or German accent, and also shared news about the most recent events of the war. Pennsylvanians had reason to pay attention. The Confederate Army wasn't far away. News of General Robert E. Lee's invasion of the North had folks in Maryland and Pennsylvania seized with fear. Rumors of Rebel behavior—stealing property, destroying homes, attacking women and children—might have been exaggerated, but how was anyone to know for sure? Many of Pittsburgh's women had no men at home, no men to protect them, and no men to provide a steady, adequate income.

Catherine Foley, a 37-year-old widow, had no one to count on except herself and her 20-year-old daughter Margaret. The two of them shared a home with an older woman named Ann McShafer, just down the street from the Allegheny Arsenal. Catherine was probably raised to believe in the ideal of the "true woman," someone who was a good wife, mother, and homemaker. In both the North and South, a true woman knew her place—and it was at home. But Catherine lost the advantages of that kind of life when her husband died, sometime before 1860. For the first time, Catherine had to step outside her home into the world of work to earn her own money. She had few options for doing respectable work. Some of the "ladies" in the lower-income neighborhoods like Catherine's worked as prostitutes, making enough money to earn a steady income. They also earned the shame-laden disapproval of other women.

In the years before the war began, Lawrenceville and other "wards" around Pittsburgh swelled with the arrival of immigrants, many of them young, female, single, and illiterate. The American-born people who lived in this area were working-class poor, the same group that made up the largest percentage of volunteer soldiers who left to join the fight in 1861. About 200 Lawrenceville women, including Catherine and Margaret Foley, were hired at the arsenal, and they all felt fortunate to have their jobs. The requirements were simple: the girls and women had to be morally upright (testified for by a prominent male citizen, such as a minister or physician), had to follow orders, and must make as many ammunition cartridges each day as their hands could produce. The ability to read and write was not necessary.

Another Catherine worked at the arsenal: 16-year-old Catherine Burkhart. Her mother and father had left Germany to build a new life in America, but her father died sometime before 1860. Like most of the poor young women in Allegheny County, Catherine was glad to have a job that would help her 50-year-old widowed mother pay the bills.

As she neared the front gate, Catherine began to focus on the day's work ahead. She and the other girls and women kicked up dust as they walked on the new stone road that the arsenal's commander, Colonel John Symington, had installed only two months before. The stones were bone dry.

WHEN AMMUNITION BECAME WOMEN'S WORK

Only six months into the war, Colonel John Symington had replaced the boys who were making cartridges at the arsenal. Up to this time, making war materials was viewed as "man's work." Teenage boys had been hired to make musket and rifle cartridges for two reasons: first, most of the men in the area had joined the Union Army and were gone and, second, their hands were smaller and more agile than older men's.

However, the boys were hard to manage. They liked to fool around. An Allegheny Arsenal supervisor found unlit matches in rooms where gunpowder was stored—most likely left there by boys sneaking a smoke. Another time, matches were found packed with cartridge bundles, another dangerous mistake.

Symington wrote to his superior: "I have discharged all the boys at work in that portion of the laboratory, and will supply their places with females."[2] He, and most other men, believed women would be easy to manage because they would obey those in charge. Local newspapers announced the open jobs, and girls and women hurried to fill them. No discipline problems occurred after this. Some boys continued to work at the laboratory, but they had specific jobs, such as sweeping up the gunpowder from the porches and roads, that kept them out of the cartridge rooms.

Soon all of the arsenals hired girls and women, in both the North and South. To allay any concerns about this work being inappropriate for women, the popular newspaper *Harper's Weekly* featured the illustration on the facing page, showing the differences between—and the harmony of—the men's work and the women's at the Watertown (Massachusetts) Arsenal. The idyllic scene gives no indication of the dangers of the job.

The women of the Watertown (Mass.) Arsenal, shown here on the cover of the popular Harper's Weekly *in 1861, worked in more crowded quarters than the men of the arsenal. The Watertown women would later protest their dangerous working conditions to their congressman, who ordered an investigation.*

None of the girls could remember the last time rain washed away the dust and excess gunpowder that seemed to settle everywhere. Finally, they all reached the three laboratory buildings between Butler Street and Penn Avenue. After leaving their bonnets and dinner bundles in the wardrobe building, the girls went to their assigned stations, stepping up on the covered porches and through the doors on the wooden buildings.

THE WOMEN AND GIRLS AT WORK: IN THE CARTRIDGE ROOMS

By 6:00 A.M., the laboratory rooms were filled with 156 women and girls. Another 30 civilian workers in the laboratory area were men or young boys. Six of the rooms—No. 1, No. 3, No. 4, No. 12, No. 13, and No. 14—were cartridge rooms. Each worker took her assigned spot on a hard wooden bench on either side of a large table. The girls sat as close to one another as they could, taking into account the wide, hooped skirts and crinolines many of them wore.

The Foley women, Catherine Burkhart, and the others unbuttoned the cuffs of their dresses and rolled up their sleeves to just below their elbows on this warm September day. They needed to keep their work dresses as clean as possible to get several days' wear out of them. Working-class families had little money to spend on extra clothing. The gunpowder, fine as flour and black as coal, would have ruined the sleeves of their dresses. Gunpowder stains were ugly, and the loose powder was dangerous. These cartridge

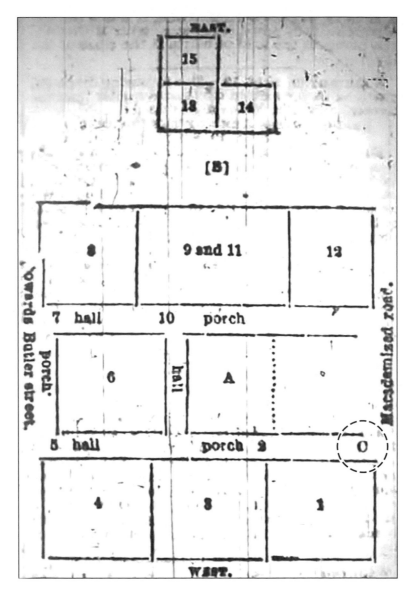

The Allegheny Arsenal, from a diagram in the Sept. 20, 1862,
issue of the Pittsburgh Dispatch, *based on the report by Superintendent*
Alexander McBride. The girls worked in laboratory rooms Nos. 1, 3, 4, 6,
and 12. McBride's office was room No. 8, across the hall from where his
daughter Kate worked. The first explosion happened at letter C, circled above.
The youngest girls were in room No. 6, the cap cylinder room.

makers knew about the dangers. They had been trained well and were often reminded by their supervisors about being careful.

Several single young women in the cartridge rooms were recent arrivals from Europe. Ellen and Mary Slattery, ages 20 and 18, had been in the U.S. for only eight years. Mary Collins, a 21-year-old from Ireland, listed her occupation as "servant" in the 1860 census, but now worked at the arsenal. Another Irish immigrant, Hester Heslip, 20, used the term "housemaid" to describe her work in 1860, but found there was more money in making cartridges for the government. Three others—Mary Murphy, age 19, Catherine Miller, age 22, and Ellen McKenna, age 19—had also been born in Ireland.

Widow Catherine Foley must have felt like a mother to these girls, and probably watched over some of them as they worked. Catherine Burkhart may have felt a kinship with Mrs. Foley's daughter, Margaret, and with Mary S. Robinson, 21, and her sister Martha, 17, because they, too, were helping their widowed mother make ends meet.

Upon the tables were all the ingredients needed to produce cartridges—the most common ammunition of the war. Cartridges held the bullets and gunpowder for muskets and rifles, weapons nearly every soldier carried. The girls' work was easy but monotonous, and special care had to be taken when working with these dangerous materials.

The supervisors had created a division of labor. The process began in the Cylinder Room, where some young women rolled paper cylinders that would become cartridges when filled. They followed to the letter the directions printed in *The Ordnance Manual for the Use of the Officers of the United States Army*. To make the cylinders, workers used a wooden dowel called a "former." It was the same width as a finished cartridge, was about seven inches long, and had a point on one end. (See illustration below.)

The women placed one of the two pieces of precut paper against the former and rolled it into a cylinder. After "choking" the pointed end closed with string, they placed

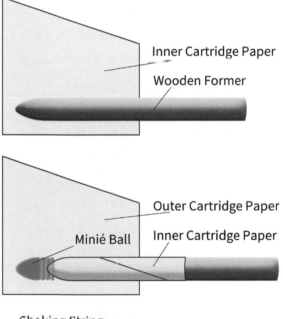

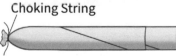

This diagram shows the three steps in making the paper cylinder and adding the minié ball. These cylinders were then taken to the filling room for gunpowder to be poured in and the cylinder folded shut, creating the finished cartridge.

Inner Cartridge Paper

Wooden Former

Outer Cartridge Paper

Minié Ball Inner Cartridge Paper

Choking String

a minié ball over the closed end of the paper (still on the wooden former) and proceeded to wrap the entire piece with the second piece of paper. It was choked closed just as before. The women then removed the former and placed the cylinder in a box.

When a box was filled, a man moved the box to the next room, the Filling Room. Women didn't move any boxes, but instead had to stay seated to continue their work at the tables. A worker had to get permission to leave the table, even for "personal" reasons.

Next, in the Filling Room, the girls used a funnel to pour a premeasured amount of gunpowder into each paper cylinder. Once filled, the worker tapped the cartridge gently to get the gunpowder to settle into the cylinder. Then she flattened the empty end of the paper and closed that end in a three-fold process.

Each girl placed her finished cartridges in a box set in front of her. The box was on its side so the girls could lay the cartridges in rows, one atop the other, until 100 cartridges filled the wooden box. Each cartridge lay flat with the bullet-end pointing toward the workers. Then these boxes were carried to another building to be packed into bundles.

The soft sound of the women's work was all that could be heard until supervisors—always men—walked through the rooms admonishing all of the women to be careful not to spill the gunpowder and to stop any chatter. Focus on work kept accidents from happening and helped produce thousands of small-arms cartridges. Each woman did the same

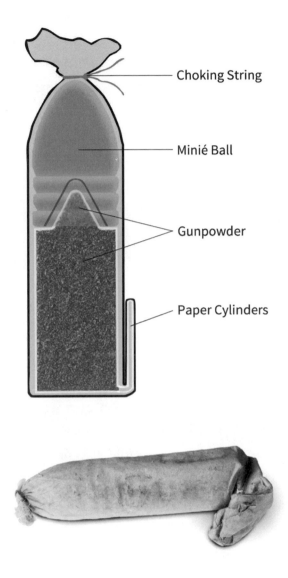

Choking String

Minié Ball

Gunpowder

Paper Cylinders

A cross-section of a finished rifle cartridge and a photo of an actual Civil War .58 caliber rifle cartridge.

job over and over again, twelve hours a day, six days a week. (At the beginning of the war, cartridge makers worked ten-hour days, but the demand for ammunition soon pushed the workday up to twelve hours.) Shoulders and backs ached, but the work had to be done, and quotas had to be met if the girls were going to keep these jobs.

THE WOMEN AND GIRLS AT WORK: ROOM NO. 6, THE CAP CYLINDER ROOM

In the Cap Cylinder Room, the smallest and youngest girls made the tiniest part of ammunition: the percussion cap. Percussion caps (shown on the next page, next to a per-cussion tube) were small pieces of metal, usually made of copper, with one closed end. Inside, the girls put a small amount of mercury fulminate (a mixture of mercury, nitric acid, and alcohol), which is highly explosive when it is struck by another object. Twelve percussion caps were placed in-side a paper tube (usually green to differentiate it from the cartridges), and the ends were folded shut to prevent the caps from falling out. For obvious reasons, percussion caps were kept away from the rooms where the gunpowder and bullets were being assembled into cartridges.

Kate McBride was one of the workers in room No. 6 this day. She was only 15, the oldest of seven children of Alexander and Virginia McBride. Her father was the super-intendent of the arsenal's laboratory. Years before, he had left Ireland for a better life, but, unlike some other men who came to America at the time, he arrived with a skill.

Percussion caps (right) and tube. Each tube usually held 12 percussion caps.

A BIT ABOUT CIVIL WAR RIFLES

Union and Confederate alike, the most common weapon was a musket or rifle. It was the weapon of choice for the infantryman, the foot soldier. Union soldiers mostly had Springfield rifles (see photo) that took a .58 caliber cartridge, loaded at the muzzle end of the barrel.

The cartridge was a paper cylinder that held a minié ball and about five ounces of gunpowder. These rifles weighed between six and ten pounds each—even more when a bayonet was attached to its barrel. These guns were notorious for being inaccurate, often shooting over the heads of their targets, and they took a long time to load. Confederate soldiers favored the Enfield rifle, made in England, which the Confederate government purchased from the English early in the conflict. Naval blockades eventually kept new shipments from reaching the Southern troops.

Cavalry soldiers, on horseback, needed weapons that would load easily, and they had both rifles and revolvers (handguns). Revolvers were tricky to load and were accurate for only about 50 feet. Their rifles, called carbines, were breech-loaded (loaded near the hammer end) and had shorter barrels. Confederate cavalrymen relied on sawed-off shotguns and hunting rifles on the battlefield.

LOADING THE AMMO ON THE BATTLEFIELD

When the boxes of cartridges got to the units on the battlefield, the bundles were distributed to the soldiers. Each man carried six bundles in his pack, providing 60 rounds of firepower.

Most muskets and rifles were muzzle-loaded. That means the ammunition was put in the muzzle of the gun, the open end of the barrel, not the breech end, near the trigger and firing mechanism. The main difference between a musket and a rifle was inside the barrel. The metal cylinder of a musket barrel was smooth inside. A rifle barrel was "rifled," thus the name. Rifled barrels were not smooth; inside grooves were cut in a spiral. These grooves made the bullet spin when it was forced through the cylinder upon firing. A spinning bullet could travel further and with more accuracy. It also left fewer dirty deposits inside the barrel—and a clean barrel meant fewer accidents.

To load the gun, a soldier took out one cartridge, tore off the folded end (often by biting and pulling), and poured the gunpowder and bullet down the barrel. The bullet held the gunpowder in. Next he pushed down the barrel with a ram-rod, securing the ammunition tightly. He placed a percussion cap at the other end to provide the spark when he fired. As you can imagine, this was not a quick process. Some tell that the best-trained soldiers could load and fire up to three shots a minute. Under the stress of battle, however, this loading speed was unlikely.

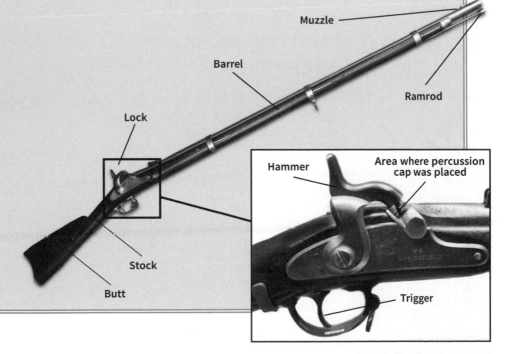

Muzzle

Barrel

Ramrod

Lock

Hammer

Area where percussion cap was placed

Stock

Butt

Trigger

He was a cooper, someone who made and repaired barrels. His experience with barrels made him useful to the arsenal. Wooden barrels filled with gunpowder were delivered regularly at the laboratory. In fact, McBride was expecting a ten-barrel delivery this day.

Kate wasn't the youngest worker at the arsenal. We don't know how many other girls were her age or younger, but we know that Mary Davison was 14, and she was at work on this day. So was her 16-year-old sister, Agnes. At home were their mother, Isabella, and father, Edward, and four other siblings (two older brothers had died before 1860). Edward Davison was a prominent man in Lawrenceville. He had built a business as a carpenter and contractor and had constructed many of the buildings in the small burg. He stayed home during the war, so why Mary and Agnes were working at the arsenal, we will never know.

THE FINAL STEP IN THE PROCESS: BUNDLES OF AMMUNITION

One by one, the gunpowder girls in the Choking Room mounded the cartridges into stacks inside the boxes on the tables. Men carried the filled boxes to the Packing Room where women counted out ten cartridges and made a double stack of five, alternating bullet up/bullet down. One cylinder that held twelve percussion caps was added before the workers wrapped each set inside waterproof paper and tied the bundle with string. The paper was labeled with information about the type of weapon the ammunition was for, the amount of gunpowder per cartridge, the name of the arsenal, the date, and the caliber of the cartridges. These cartridge bundles were placed snugly inside wooden boxes. Each of these boxes held 1,000 rounds of ammunition—100 bundles. Filled boxes were screwed shut and painted with a waterproof material. Boxes were marked with the date and the arsenal's name. They were stored in other buildings at the laboratory and eventually sent to the battlefield. The ladies of Lawrenceville worked Monday through Saturday, completing about 128,000 cartridges a day, and earning between $.50 and $1.20 each for twelve hours' work, less than half what the men before them had earned. But today was payday. The girls were eager to collect their cash payment during the dinner break and take it home that evening. For a few minutes, they could take their minds off the dangerous work and relax.

Chapter Two

THE BLOODIEST DAY OF THE WAR

As THE SUN MOVED HIGH IN A CLOUDLESS SKY, THE DAY GREW EVEN WARMER. It had been more than a month since any rain had fallen. By noon, the girls were ready to stretch their backs, arms, and legs. They kept working, though, pushing to fulfill more than half of the day's quota before taking their dinner break. Quotas had been increased recently because of the heavy fighting in Maryland, a state that shared a border with Pennsylvania and had never declared its position in the war. Confederate General Robert E. Lee had invaded Maryland, and rumors of a major battle to come spread quickly.

Northerners worried that Lee's troops might continue into other states, especially Pennsylvania. A dismal summer of Union losses caused the government to call for more arms and ammunition. Patriotic workers did their best to meet the demand, especially at the Allegheny Arsenal. This very morning—though no one in Lawrenceville knew it yet—Union and Rebel troops had begun heavy fighting near Sharpsburg, Maryland, along Antietam Creek.

Around 1:00 P.M., supervisors began excusing workers at the Allegheny Arsenal to take their midday break. When they finished their meal, the girls stood in line to get paid. One by one, they placed their mark on the payroll ledger and received their money. The August ledger showed how many cartridges each girl had helped complete in July, and her pay was based on that number. This is known as piece-work. Each girl earned 18 cents per 1,000 cartridges made. Most of the girls made less than $20 per month. The payroll ledger shown on the next page tells us that Mary Robinson earned $17.28 for the 96,000 cartridges she had helped make in July.

ONE SINGLE SPARK

As they stood in line, the girls heard the clip-clop-clip-clop of horses' hooves on the stone road just beyond the laboratory buildings. Joseph Frick was busy delivering ten barrels of gunpowder to the area. Each barrel weighed 100 pounds. He stopped outside Room No. 1 to drop off three barrels, and then moved on to the front of Room No. 12, where five barrels were unloaded and put on the porch. The last two were placed in front of Room No. 13 and No. 14. After getting her pay, each of the girls returned to her station to finish out the day's work.

The August 1862 payroll records for the Allegheny Arsenal women shows the names of many of the victims, the number of cartridges each one completed, and total pay for their work in July.

It was about 2:00 P.M. Some were still in the pay line, waiting their turn. They were the lucky ones.

Frick turned his wagon around and headed the horses back down the road in front of the laboratory buildings, gaining speed as he was leaving. Robert Smith, age 37, stood beside the gunpowder barrels in front of Room No. 1. Rachel Dunlap watched as the horses pulled the wagon past the shed between Room No. 1 and Room No. 12. Then she saw it. A spark from one of the horse's metal shoes, just in front of the wagon wheel, ignited a patch of loose gunpowder on the roadway. A thin artery of flames moved from the road and flowed in a stream of fire, following a black path to the porch of Room No. 1.

Three barrels. Three full barrels of gunpowder sat there as the flames raced toward them.

Suddenly, a violent explosion threw fire and wood in all directions. Robert Smith was killed instantly. The wagon driver, Frick, was thrown from his seat, but not badly injured. One of the horses was burned.

The girls in Rooms 1, 3, and 4 screamed in terror as the air around them filled with heat, fire, and exploding cartridges. Many of them were horribly burned, and others were blown to pieces, as one room's fire spread to the others. Girls ran from the rooms, their clothes covered in flames, and they screamed as the fire devoured their clothing. Male workers rushed into the rooms to rescue girls trapped under fallen debris.

Superintendent Alexander McBride was in his office in Room 8 when he heard the explosion. He ran to Room 6 where his daughter, Kate, was working. The fire had already taken hold, and just as he got there, the roof collapsed on the room. Four of the nine girls inside had escaped before the collapse, but Kate was not one of them. He was too late.

Joseph Bollman, age 42, pulled a girl from the room, saving her life. McBride recalled,

> **"I got on to the window at the end of the room; fell out, and having got out of the dust or flame, returned along the side of the laboratory to room #6, to seek my daughter; got on the porch and met Joseph E. Bollman with a girl on his arm coming out. At the same time, I saw the ceiling of room #6, falling on the floor where the children were. The flames and dust forced me back. Mr. Bollman let down the child he had upon the porch, and near the fences I saw a girl bewildered, with her clothes burnt off."[3]**

Bollman went back inside, trying to save more girls. There is no doubt that he was looking for his daughter, Mary, age 15. Neither of them would survive the disaster.

Loose gunpowder on the adjoining porches continued to ignite, and five minutes later, a second explosion erupted when the fire reached the five barrels near Room No. 12. This explosion, much greater than the first, destroyed the rest of the laboratory. This explosion killed more girls and some of the men who were trying to save them.

It took only one minute for the third and final explosion to happen, probably caused by fiery debris landing on or near the two barrels of gunpowder near Room No. 14. The fire continued to consume the buildings and the girls who couldn't escape. Inside the rooms, thousands of rounds of ammunition exploded, sending bullets and lead fragments everywhere. Pieces of the girls' and women's bodies flew into the air, landing in the yard and in the trees nearby. Girls ran from the rooms, their bodies aflame and their faces burned black. Men tried to extinguish the fire on their dresses by covering them with coats, shirts, or whatever they could find.

One of the workers, young Mary Jane Black, described what she saw as she returned from getting her pay. Upon hearing screams, Mary Jane turned and saw "two girls behind me; they were on fire; their faces were burning and blood was running from them. I pulled the clothes off one of them; while I was doing this, the other one ran up and begged me to cover her."[4]

From the moment the first explosion was heard, people flocked to the site, drawn by the column of smoke that rose above the arsenal. At first, some feared that the Confederate Army had attacked, but soon the word spread that a horrible accident had happened. Family members of the girls who worked there were desperate to find their daughters or sisters and to hear that they were safe. One reporter wrote that he heard "agonizing screams of relatives and friends upon discovering the remains of some loved one whose humble earnings contributed to their comfort."[5]

The primary newspaper of the area, the *Pittsburgh Gazette*, described the scene in remarkable detail the following day:

> **On reaching the place, an appalling sight was present-**
> **ed. The large building, known as the Laboratory, . . . was**
> **laid in ruins—having been heaved up by the force of the**
> **explosion, and then fallen in fragments, after which it**
> **caught fire and was consumed, the flames still being in**
> **progress when we arrived there. . . . [T]he dead bodies**
> **were seen lying in heaps, just as they had fallen when**
> **the explosion took place.**
>
> **In some parts, where the heat was intense, nothing but**
> **the whitened bones could be seen, while in other places**
> **large masses of blacked flesh were visible amidst the**
> **smoke.**[6]

Everything was chaos. Firemen scrambled to extinguish any flames or sparks that might cause the disaster to spread further. Men pulled Lawrenceville's new fire truck (which had been in service for only five days) up a hill to a nearby pond for water and did what they could to extinguish the flames. Bucket lines were formed, adding to the effort.

In the midst of the chaos, relatives scrambled over smoldering debris, looking for their loved ones, scanning the scene for some sight of a familiar face or fabric or shoe— anything to help them identify the bodies on the ground.

But not many clues remained. Piles of ashes lay where workers had once stood, leaving only the metal hoops of the girls' crinolines. Shoes and stockings were strewn here and there, but no one was in them. One man was identified only by his false teeth. Some body parts were found hanging from trees in the area, and others were later found far from the buildings, as far away as the Allegheny River, about half a mile north of the explosion. The concussion of the explosions broke windows in all directions. Some said the blast was heard and felt three miles away.

DETERMINING A DEATH COUNT

Soon a list began to take shape: the dead, the missing, the injured. Workers guessed that more than 70 people were killed, but it would take weeks to come up with a definitive list. Even so, the *Pittsburgh Gazette* began to name the fallen, according to the information they were given by families or employers at the arsenal. Some sources list Kate Dillon as the youngest of those killed. She was only 10 years old. Her sister Ann perished, too.

Over the next two days, workers and relatives continued looking for, and finding, victims of the disaster. Wooden planks were laid down, and the dead and mortally wounded were placed on them. The injured workers who had a chance of survival were treated and moved to makeshift hospital rooms in nearby houses or to their own homes for care.

The Pittsburgh Gazette reported that someone had found the bodies of Mary Algeo, 15, and Ellen Rushton, 21, the day after the explosion, "in Union Park, on the other side of the turnpike, and two or three hundred yards from the scene of the disaster." The newspaper said that Miss Algeo "was still alive when found, but expired soon after."[7] She had lain there for more than 24 hours before being found. Ellen Rushton was dead at the scene.

Family members took the girls' bodies back to their homes. When relatives were able to identify a deceased loved one, they took the body home to prepare the victim for burial, as was common in that day. The women and girls whose remains were identified were buried in marked graves at one of the two cemeteries in the county: the Allegheny Cemetery (for Protestants) and St. Mary Cemetery (for Catholics). For the remaining unidentified dead, the government provided 39 black wooden coffins. The Allegheny Cemetery donated a parcel of land where these coffins were buried in a mass grave. No known public ceremony took place, and it would be more than a year before any monument marked that site. The original monument deteriorated, and a new marker with the names of the victims replaced it in 1928 (see photo on page 45).

Over the next two weeks, a few more victims died of their injuries, especially those who were severely burned, adding to the list of the dead. The final count was 78. Half of those bodies were never identified, so the coroner depended on attendance records for that day to name those victims. About 70 more were injured but survived. Most of the dead and injured were girls and young women.

THE WORST DAY OF THE WAR

September 17, 1862, was the deadliest day of the American Civil War—on two fronts. The Battle of Antietam lasted more than ten hours and claimed the lives of more than 3,600 soldiers, with a total casualty count of more than 22,000.[8] To this day, it is remembered as the bloodiest day in American history.

Not far away, near Pittsburgh, Pennsylvania, on the very same day, the Allegheny Arsenal explosion killed 78 civilians. It was the worst civilian disaster of the war.

Newspapers around the country carried the reports of Antietam, but few recounted the events at the Allegheny Arsenal.

INSCRIPTION FROM ORIGINAL MONUMENT

ERECTED BY VOLUNTARY SUBSCRIPTION TO THE MEMORY OF THOSE WHO WERE KILLED BY THE EXPLOSION AT THE ALLEGHENY ARSENAL, SEPTEMBER 17, 1862. TREAD SOFTLY, THIS IS CONSECRATED DUST. FORTY FIVE PURE PATRIOTIC VICTIMS LIE HERE, A SACRIFICE TO FREEDOM AND CIVIL LIBERTY, A HORRID MEMENTO OF A MOST WICKED REBELLION. PATRIOTS! THESE ARE PATRIOTS' GRAVES, FRIENDS OF HUMBLE HONEST TOIL, THESE WERE YOUR PEERS. FERVENT AFFECTION KINDLED THESE HEARTS, HONEST INDUSTRY EMPLOYED THESE HANDS. WIDOWS' AND ORPHANS' TEARS HAVE WATERED THIS GROUND. FEMALE BEAUTY AND MANHOOD'S VIGOR COMMINGLE HERE. IDENTIFIED BY MAN, KNOWN BY HIM WHO IS THE RESURRECTION AND THE LIFE, TO BE MADE KNOWN AND LOVED AGAIN, WHEN THE MORNING COMETH.

ELIZABETH AGER	MELINDA COLSTON	DAVID GILLILAND	ELIZABETH J. MAXWELL	MARGARET O'ROURKE
MARY ALGEO	MARY CRANAN	VIRGINIA HAMMILL	SARAH A. MAXWELL	MARY RIORDAN
MARY AMARINE	AGNES M. DAVISON	SIDNEY HANLON	ELLA McAFEE	MARTHA ROBINSON
HANNAH BAXTER	MARY A. DAVISON	MARY J. HEENY	KATE McBRIDE	MARY ROBINSON
BARBARA BISHOP	ANN DILLON	HESTER HESLIP	MARIA McCARTHY	MARY S. ROBINSON
JOSEPH E. BOLLMAN	KATE DILLON	MARY J. JEFFREY	SUSAN McCREIGHT	NANCY ROSS
MARY A. BOLLMAN	KATE DONAHUE	MRS. MARY J. JOHNSON	ELLEN McKENNA	ELLA RUSHTON
ROSE BRADY	SARAH DONNELL	ANNIE JONES	SUSAN McKENNA	ELEANOR SHEPARD
ELLA BROWN	MARY DONNELLY	CATHERINE KALER	GRACE McMILLAN	SARAH SHEPARD
ALICE BURIE	MAGDALENE DOUGLAS	MARGARET KELLEY	ANDREW McWHIRTER	ELIZABETH SHOOK
SARAH BURKE	MARY A. DRIPPS	URIAH LAUGHLIN	MARY ANN McWHIRTER	ELLEN SLATTERY
CATHERINE BURKHART	CATHERINE DUGAN	ELIZA LINDSAY	CATHERINE MILLER	MARY SLATTERY
BRIDGET CLARE	NANCY FLEMING	HARRIET LINDSAY	PHILLIP MILLER	ROBERT SMITH
EMMA CLOWES	CATHERINE FOLEY	ADALINE MAHRER	MARY MURPHY	LUCINDA TRUXALL
MARY COLLINS	SUSAN FRITCHLEY	ELLEN MANCHESTER	MELINDA NECKERMAN	MARGARET A. TURNEY
	SARAH GEORGE	ELIZABETH MARKLE	ALICE NUGENT	

THIS MONUMENT ERECTED UNDER THE AUSPICES OF SONS OF UNION VETERANS OF THE CIVIL WAR AND THE LADIES AUXILIARY OF THIS ORGANIZATION — DEDICATED MAY 27, 1928

INSCRIPTION FROM ORIGINAL MONUMENT

ERECTED BY VOLUNTARY SUBSCRIPTION TO THE MEMORY OF THOSE WHO WERE KILLED BY THE EXPLOSION AT THE ALLEGHENY ARSENAL, SEPTEMBER 17, 1862. TREAD SOFTLY, THIS IS CONSECRATED DUST. FORTY FIVE PURE PATRIOTIC VICTIMS LIE HERE, A SACRIFICE TO FREEDOM AND CIVIL LIBERTY, A HORRID MEMENTO OF A MOST WICKED REBELLION. THESE ARE PATRIOTS' GRAVES, FRIENDS OF HUMBLE HONEST TOIL, THESE WERE YOUR PEERS. FERVENT AFFECTION KINDLED THESE HEARTS, HONEST INDUSTRY EMPLOYED THESE HANDS. WIDOWS' AND ORPHANS' TEARS HAVE WATERED THIS GROUND, FEMALE BEAUTY AND MANHOOD'S VIGOR COMMINGLE HERE. IDENTIFIED BY MAN, KNOWN BY HIM WHO IS THE RESURRECTION AND THE LIFE, TO BE MADE KNOWN AND LOVED AGAIN, WHEN THE MORNING COMETH.

ELIZABETH AGER, MARY ALGEO, MARY AMARINE, HANNAH BAXTER, BARBARA BISHOP, JOSEPH E. BOLLMAN, MARY A. BOLLMAN, ROSE BRADY, ELLA BROWN, ALICE BURIE, SARAH BURKE, CATHERINE BURKHART, BRIDGET CLARE, EMMA CLOWES, MARY COLLINS, MELINDA COLSTON, MARY CRANAN, AGNES M. DAVISON, MARY A. DAVISON, ANN DILLON, KATE DILLON, KATE DONAHUE, SARAH DONNELL, MARY DONNELLY, MAGDALENE DOUGLAS, MARY A. DRIPPS, CATHERINE DUGAN, NANCY FLEMING, CATHERINE FOLEY, SUSAN FRITCHLEY, SARAH GEORGE, DAVID GILLILAND, VIRGINIA HAMMILL, SIDNEY HANLON, MARY J. HEENY, HESTER HESLIP, MARY J. JEFFREY, MRS. MARY J. JOHNSON, ANNIE JONES, CATHERINE KALER, MARGARET KELLEY, URIAH LAUGHLIN, ELIZA LINDSAY, HARRIET LINDSAY, ADALINE MAHRER, ELLEN MANCHESTER, ELIZABETH MARKLE, ELIZABETH J. MAXWELL, SARAH A. MAXWELL, ELLA McAFEE, KATE McBRIDE, MARIA McCARTHY, SUSAN McCREIGHT, ELLEN McKENNA, SUSAN McKENNA, GRACE McMILLAN, ANDREW McWHIRTER, MARY ANN McWHIRTER, CATHERINE MILLER, PHILLIP MILLER, MARY MURPHY, MELINDA NECKERMAN, ALICE NUGENT, MARGARET O'ROURKE, MARY RIORDAN, MARTHA ROBINSON, MARY ROBINSON, MARY S. ROBINSON, NANCY ROSS, ELLA RUSHTON, ELEANOR SHEPARD, SARAH SHEPARD, ELIZABETH SHOOK, ELLEN SLATTERY, MARY SLATTERY, ROBERT SMITH, LUCINDA TRUXALL, MARGARET A. TURNEY

A memorial stands in the Allegheny Cemetery at the mass grave where half of the victims were laid to rest. All 78 names appear on the front of the marker.

DEATHS CAUSED BY THE ALLEGHENY ARSENAL EXPLOSION

(Ages and family relationships are based on 1860 U.S. Census records‡)

Name (relationship)	Age	Name (relationship)	Age
Elizabeth Ager*	20	Mary Donnelly*	19
Mary Algeo	15	Magdalene Douglas*	16
Mary Amarine	15	Mary Dripps*	unknown
Hannah Baxter	21	Catherine Dugan	42
Barbara Bishop	17	Nancy Fleming*	17
Joseph Bollman* (father)	42	Catherine Foley	37
Mary Bollman* (daughter)	15	Susan Fritchley*	unknown
Rose Brady*	unknown	Sarah George*	unknown
Ella Brown*	unknown	David Gilliland*	58
Alice Burke (sister)	unknown	Virginia Hammill*	unknown
Sarah Burke* (sister)	15	Sidney Hanlon	14
Catherine Burkhart	16	Mary Heeney*	unknown
Bridget Clare*	unknown	Hester Heslip	20
Emma Clowes*	unknown	Mary Jeffrey	37
Mary Collins*	21	Mary Johnson	unknown
Melinda Colston*	15	Annie Jones	unknown
Mary Cranan	15	Catherine Kaler*	20
Agnes Davison* (sister)	16	Margaret Kelley	29
Mary Davison* (sister)	14	Uriah Laughlin	33
Ann Dillon*	unknown	Elizabeth Lindsay*	17
Kate Dillon	10	Harriet Lindsay*	28
Kate Donahue*	unknown	Adaline Mahrer*	unknown
Sarah Donnell	unknown		

Name (relationship)	Age	Name (relationship)	Age
Ellen Manchester*	22	Melinda Neckerman*	unknown
Elizabeth Markle*	16	Alice Nugent	26
Elizabeth Maxwell (sister)	19	Margaret O'Rourke	18
Sarah Maxwell (sister)	24	Mary Riordan	unknown
Ella McAfee	unknown	Martha Robinson (sister)	17
Kate McBride	15	Mary S. Robinson* (sister)	21
Maria McCarthy*	20	Nancy Ross	unknown
Susan McCreight*	unknown	Ella Rushton	21
Ellen McKenna	19	Eleanor Shepard	unknown
Susan McKenna	18	Sarah Shepard*	17
Grace McMillan	unknown	Elizabeth Shook	unknown
Andrew McWhirter	unknown	Ellen Slattery (sister)	20
Mary A. McWhirter*	22	Mary Slattery (sister)	18
Catherine Miller*	22	Robert Smith*	37
Phillip Miller	14	Lucinda Truxall	16
Mary Murphy*	19	Margaret Turney*	15

‡ Age is determined based on 1860 U.S. Census records and assumes that a birthday has already occurred in 1862. Not all names were found in records. I did not make assumptions about family ties based on the same surname; only those whose records I found are marked as sisters or father/daughter.

* Indicates body was unidentifiable and buried in mass grave.

Chapter Three

WHAT WENT WRONG: THE INVESTIGATION

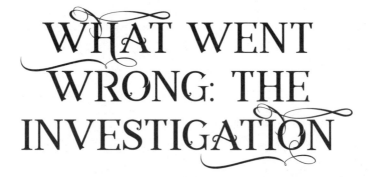

THE LABORATORY BUILDINGS LAY IN RUINS. Likewise, families were devastated when they discovered their loved ones were never coming home again. Some suffered a double blow to learn that pairs of sisters were among the dead, and in one case, a father and daughter. As hundreds of people mourned, an investigation into the catastrophe began.

The county coroner was John McClung. It was his job to convene a coroner's inquest, creating a jury of men to hear testimony about the cause of the explosion. His jury was ready to begin questioning witnesses the next morning, Thursday, September 18. He had three reasons for starting the proceedings so quickly. First, despite the emotions that were still high, fresh memories of what happened were critical to discovering the cause of the explosions. Second, the U.S. was at war with an enemy who was knocking at the front door of northern territory. It was possible that this was an act of war and not a workplace accident. Finally, the sooner this tragedy could be evaluated, the sooner the arsenal could get back to work supplying the troops with ammunition. Leaders at the arsenal put personal tragedy aside and looked at the bigger picture. In fact, the following notice was published in the *Pittsburgh Gazette* that very day. The words made it clear to any southern sympathizers that the Union forces would not be diminished in any way by this unfortunate event.

> **Lest parties abroad should misapprehend the facts, it is necessary to say that but a very small fraction of the Allegheny Arsenal has been destroyed. The loss of material is nothing compared to the loss of life. The Arsenal, with its immense shops, stores, and munitions, may be said to be uninjured, and the Government will experience but a very slight interruption to its business in consequences of the accident.[9]**

TESTIMONY FROM THE WITNESSES

Commander of the arsenal, Col. Symington, allowed the investigation to commence, even though he didn't have to do so. As a military establishment, the arsenal was not a civilian property, so such an investigation could have been rejected. He agreed to cooperate because he believed understanding the cause was necessary—not only to the officers at the arsenal, so they might prevent a future disaster,

*Col. John Symington, commander of
the Allegheny Arsenal*

but also for the mourning community so the families could better understand what happened.

He most likely expected the cause to be either an accident without anyone at fault or the result of the behavior of one of the laboratory workers, maybe one of those boys with some matches. One by one, the witnesses described what they had seen the day before.

Wagon driver Joseph Frick said he saw a flame shoot up from between his horse's rear foot and the wagon wheel directly behind it.

Rachel Dunlap, a worker on dinner break who was walking on the porch of Room No. 12, confirmed Frick's testimony. She said that she saw the spark and the ensuing flame that lit the gunpowder barrels.

Another witness, William Baxter, was asked about the road beside the laboratory. He stated that, as a quarry worker, he knew that the stone road was a bad idea. In his experience, that exact kind of stone would spark if metal struck it.

Laboratory worker Elias McClure testified that Superintendent McBride was lax in making the boys sweep up and gather the loose gunpowder. Instead, the boys swept it out into the roadway.

Col. Symington and Superintendent McBride were also questioned, but neither of them had seen the first explosion happen. They could only guess at the reason for the initial cause.

After some discussion, the jury came to a divided decision. Three of the five men—the majority—ruled that the fault lay with Col. Symington and his two lieutenants, J. R. Edie and Jasper Myers, as well as Superintendent McBride and his assistant, James Thorp. The other two jurors, however, felt that Symington and his men were in no way guilty, and they placed all responsibility for the disaster on McBride and Thorp.

Col. Symington took issue with the majority decision, and he asked for a military investigation to be held that might replace the civilian ruling. One month later, witnesses had to recall and describe again the horrors of that day when they were questioned by a military court. Families had to relive the terrible details, and their words were recorded in the local newspapers. In a clear case of conflict of interest, Col. Symington acted as the court's prosecutor and worked hard to discount any testimony that blamed him or his stone road for the disaster. Instead, he pushed a story that lay all of the blame on the first victim, Robert Smith. Symington posed the possibility that Smith had jumped on top of one of the gunpowder barrels, causing a spark that ignited the powder inside. No witness ever described seeing such a thing.

One other bit of information came to light in both inquests, and it pointed outside the arsenal completely—and toward the DuPont Company. DuPont made the barrels in which the gunpowder was shipped and stored. Alexander McBride, an expert in barrel-making, had complained about the barrels long before the explosion. He was concerned that the same barrels were being reused, over and over again. The dry powder and hot storage conditions could cause the barrels to expand, causing small cracks to open between the wooden boards. Such fine powder, as gunpowder is, could sift through these cracks and fall out. That loose powder in combination with jostling wagons that carried the barrels over the roadways could cause the gunpowder to fall between the stones and even inside the rooms when the barrels were brought inside. Symington agreed that some of the blame should be placed on DuPont.

At the end of the military investigation, people were surprised when Col. Symington and his lieutenants were cleared of any responsibility in the disaster. All of the guilt was placed on Alexander McBride and James Thorp.

What was more surprising, then, was what happened over the next few weeks. Col. Symington was relieved of his command at the Allegheny Arsenal, and his two lieutenants were transferred to other posts. Alexander McBride continued to serve as the arsenal's superintendent for many years. He never spoke of the incident—or of Kate—again. His family said he never got over the loss of his daughter.

THE AFTERMATH

The government never offered any compensation for the loss of these souls, so some of the families made direct requests for help. These men, women, and children were government workers, and they were essential earners for their families. Every request was rejected. Local churches and relief groups raised some money for the victims' families.

Less than two weeks after the disaster, Reverend Richard Lea spoke about the tragedy in his Sunday sermon. His church, the Lawrenceville Presbyterian Church, was close enough to the arsenal that the percussion from the blasts blew out some of its windows. He spoke of some of the girls who had attended his church, and left visitors with a general warning: One never knows the hour when death will come.

New ads were placed calling for arsenal workers. As if the horrors had never happened, girls and women lined up to fill those jobs. The war continued to use up millions of cartridges, and people still needed to earn a living.

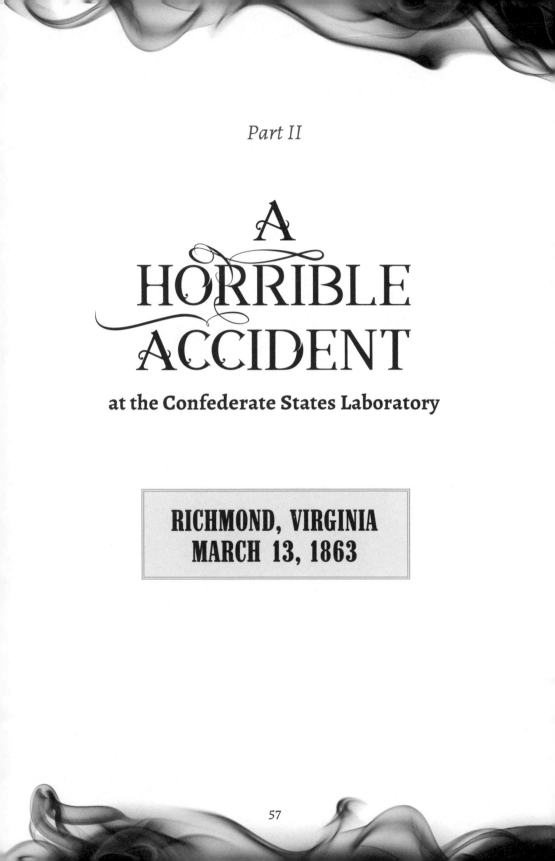

Part II

A HORRIBLE ACCIDENT

at the Confederate States Laboratory

RICHMOND, VIRGINIA
MARCH 13, 1863

Chapter Four

A FRIDAY THE THIRTEENTH

SIX MONTHS AFTER THAT FATEFUL DAY AT THE ALLEGHENY ARSENAL, THE WAR THAT WAS EXPECTED TO BE OVER QUICKLY WAS STILL GOING STRONG. The need for more and more ammunition was a grim reminder that the violence and suffering showed no signs of diminishing. It had been almost two years since the first shots of the war had been fired. The South was still determined to win its sovereignty, but the North was equally set on holding the nation together. No clear winner was emerging yet.

Some cracks were beginning to show, however. After a long winter and an effective Union blockade that kept materials from moving into the South, the Confederate economy was hurting. Soldiers and civilians alike felt the pinch. Pay and provisions caught up with the men slowly—when they came at all. Confederate troops scavenged northern towns in Maryland and Pennsylvania and took what they needed, sometimes more. Soldiers wearing ratty clothes and boots that barely covered their feet ransacked shops and homes looking for food, shoes, hats, clothing, blankets, guns, and horses. Their desperation became notorious among folks in Maryland and Pennsylvania and kept alive rumors of invasion by Rebel fighting forces.

In Richmond, Virginia, the capital of the Confederate government, the times were desperate, too. A lack of food and other essentials had driven prices way up. Families could not afford to keep their children fed, and the number of working-class poor residents was growing. Like in the North, many of these people were immigrants from Ireland, who remembered famine from their past but hoped for a better future in America. The malnourished people became an easy target for smallpox when an epidemic swept through Richmond in early 1863. As spring approached, people were looking forward to airing out their homes and planting gardens where they could.

Despite all of the winter's setbacks, the women of Richmond (so many of the men were away) supported the Confederate troops in the same ways Northern women did. Middle- and upper-class ladies sewed and knitted and cooked. They sent packages to their sons and husbands and to soldiers they had never met. They managed events that raised money for the cause. Working-class girls had to do what they'd always had to do: find a job that paid enough to keep them and their families housed and fed. Some of them found work at the local arsenal making cartridges and cannon primers. Side-by-side, cartridges for a Union rifle and those for a Confederate one were practically identical, and so were the places and the method for producing them.

The Confederate States Laboratory was also like the Allegheny Arsenal—most of its small-arms ammunition workers were young immigrant girls. Because almost all Southern men were serving the Rebel cause (as much as three-fourths of the male population), hiring women was essential to meeting the military's demands. The need was so great that girls as young as nine years old worked there.

FROM SEVENTH STREET TO BROWN'S ISLAND

The Confederate States Laboratory was also known as the Richmond Arsenal. It didn't exist before 1861, unlike many other arsenals that had been in operation for decades. As the strain between the North and South grew, military leaders in Virginia's capital made plans to build a facility that would produce most of the weapons and ammunition needed for the fight. Captain Wesley N. Smith came to Richmond with a big job to do: set up the laboratory, hire some workers, and train them thoroughly. He took over some tobacco factory buildings at the end of Seventh Street, near the James River, to begin operations.

Captain Smith preached and practiced safety. In June 1861, soon after the arsenal opened, about 250 girls and women made small-arms cartridges in one of the buildings. Some Richmond citizens voiced concern about housing a munitions laboratory. In a *Richmond Whig* editorial, the newspaper's editors were worried that a large building, like those warehouses, held too many workers in one place. The editors suggested that it might be better if separate, smaller buildings should be used, thus reducing the chances of a horrible accident claiming hundreds of lives. Two small explosions followed, one on September 26, 1861, and the other on January 27, 1862. In the first, no one was hurt, but some women panicked and fled from the building. In the second, two young men were badly burned and died within a week of the accident. These events reminded the public of the newspaper's call for safer workplaces to be made.

After the second explosion, C. S. Laboratory leaders began work to relocate the laboratory to Brown's Island in the James River. A bridge connected the mainland to the island, and small wood-frame buildings were constructed there. All of the newspapers were invited to tour the new facilities, and none were disappointed.

The *Richmond Dispatch* described the finished setting in their January 2, 1863, edition:

> **Government Works. – The Confederate Government have [sic] established quite a settlement on Brown's Island, a place formerly devoted to cock fighting and similar amusements, and have now nearly three hundred females employed in the workshops located on the island, making up ball cartridges and other small ammunition. The place wears quite a thriving aspect.[1]**

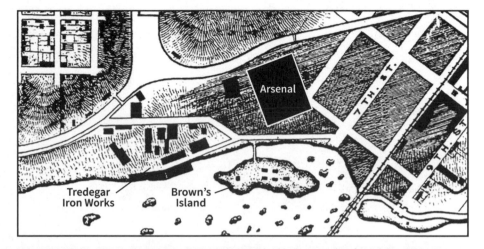

Richmond Arsenal, also known as C.S. Laboratory, with Brown's Island to the south and Tredegar Iron Works to the west. The photo below shows the bridge that spanned the James River, connecting Richmond to Brown's Island on the left.

DID SLAVE OR FREE AFRICAN-AMERICAN WOMEN WORK AT THE ARSENALS?

More than two dozen arsenals were in operation to supply both the Union and Confederate armies with guns and ammunition. Both free African-American males in the North and enslaved males in the South worked to produce materials for the soldiers. The Tredegar Iron Works in Richmond, Virginia, leased hundreds of enslaved men from their owners to help make cannons and shells. As an incentive to work hard and meet their quotas, sometimes these workers were paid cash bonuses, a bit of spending money for tobacco, food, or clothing. Mining companies put the men to work to unearth lead and iron, too. In the North, free African-Americans found jobs in the arsenals, working mainly as carpenters, blacksmiths, machinists, and general laborers.

The role of African-American women, enslaved and free, is not as easy to discern. Based on this author's research, none of the victims of the three disasters described in this book was African-American. (Census information makes it relatively easy to discover someone's race—there is a column on the forms to specify the race of each person.) However, it is likely that some of the other female workers at the Washington Arsenal were African-American, because the capital had a large, mostly free black population of about 75,000 in 1860.

In the South, records show that slave owners hired out some of their enslaved females to work in nearby arsenals. In Arkansas, two women—Mary and Flora—worked to make cartridges, and two others—Eliza and Maria—were cooks at the Arkadelphia Arsenal. Their owner, Thomas Swift, leased 41 of his enslaved men and women to work there. It is likely his plantation was either occupied by Union troops or destroyed, so he used leasing these people as a way to make money.

Rather than working in the arsenals making cartridges, however, it was much more common for both free and enslaved African-American women to work as seamstresses, outfitting the soldiers in their blue or gray uniforms. Free women volunteered as teachers to educate the newly freed African-Americans, and by 1864, about 3,000 African-American women served as nurses. Some even became scouts and spies to help the Union cause.

Susie King Taylor (shown here in 1902) was born a slave in Georgia and was raised by her grandmother in Savannah. During the war, she fled to St. Simons Island for safety under the protection of Union troops there. In 1862 Taylor became the first black teacher for freed African-American students, teaching at a Freedmen's school in Georgia. She also became the first black Army nurse, serving the troops of the 33rd U.S. Colored Infantry Regiment.

Declared as "the general ordnance manufactory of the South," the new C. S. Laboratory was celebrated for its productivity and attention to safety issues. More than 300 girls walked over the bridge each day to go to work in six buildings. Most of them worked in No. 1, No. 3, and No. 6. The girls in building No. 1 worked on percussion caps, friction primers, fuses, and rockets. (A "rocket" in Civil War terms was similar to a bottle rocket. They were inaccurate and not used much.)

In building No. 3, the girls made small-arms cartridges, following the same process as the workers at the Allegheny Arsenal. Those working in building No. 6 made ammunition for pistols and breech-loading rifles. All of these girls were well-trained and supervised by men. On average, each worker produced 1,200 cartridges each day. She earned about 40 dollars a month. (Confederate dollars tended to be inflated because of the economy in the South.)

MARCH 13, 1863–FRIDAY THE THIRTEENTH

Work on Brown's Island never lagged, and, in fact, was increased from six days a week to seven by March 1863. The girls and women kept their small hands busy filling cartridges with gunpowder and tying bundles of ammunition together. Mid-March was still cold, and the girls were grateful for the furnaces that safely piped heat into their buildings. They probably chatted or sang songs to keep their minds off the war, even as they were making the ammunition that fueled it. Everyone in Richmond realized that Union forces were never far away.

Friday, March 13th, started out like any other workday. Still, the superstitious girls may have said an extra prayer that morning or may have made the sign of the cross on their way to work. Some may not have even been aware of the date at all. No matter. There was so much to get done by the time the sun went down.

Sisters walked together and friends came alongside as they converged at the bridge just after dawn. Once they stepped onto the island, they separated into work groups and headed to their posts. Mary Ryan, age 18, was one of the older girls and an Irish immigrant. She went to building No. 6, as usual.

The number of workers assigned to that building had recently changed. While another building was being enlarged, some of the girls from it were moved to No. 6, so a variety of unrelated tasks were carried out under one roof. At one table, some girls were filling empty paper cartridges with gunpowder and minié balls, tying them closed, and placing them in boxes. At the same long table, others were removing cannon friction primers from boards so they could be packaged and sent to the battlefield. That was Mary Ryan's job.

Also in building No. 6, but at a separate table, girls dismantled faulty cartridges that had been returned. They opened the paper cylinders and made two piles on the table: one of gunpowder and one of minié balls. Particles of the soft, black powder floated in the air.

WHAT IS A FRICTION PRIMER?

In a time long before tanks and airplanes, the biggest war machine was the cannon. Hundreds of cannons, weighing between 200 and 2,000 pounds, moved with the Union and Confederate armies in the Civil War. Alongside these rolling guns were artillery wagons filled with the three supplies necessary to make a cannon useful in battle: cannon balls or shells, gunpowder, and friction primers. Friction primers were small, metal tubes that produced a tiny spark. That spark ignited a bag of gunpowder inside the cannon, which created an explosion that propelled balls or shells (some as heavy as 20 pounds) more than a mile. Like all other weapon-related materials, the friction primers were produced, packaged, stored, and shipped from arsenals.

Each primer had three main components: a long, metal tube; gunpowder; and a pin. Gunpowder filled the tube, and the pin—made of a material that would spark—was carefully inserted into holes at the top of the tube. A small wire was attached to a hole on the end of the pin and then wound into the shape seen here. Each primer was sealed with wax. Next, several of them were placed on a board to be sprayed with varnish, making them waterproof. These boards, when dry, were given to workers so the individual primers could be removed from the boards and packaged for shipment.

At about 10:45 A.M., one of the supervisors, Mr. McCarthy, made his usual rounds, checking on the girls and reminding them about working quickly but safely. He had a reputation for being overly concerned about safety. As he stepped beside Mary Ryan, he pointedly told her to be careful. Her work was particularly dangerous, and Mary had been warned before when she tried to bang loose some primers that were stuck on a varnish board. Satisfied that he had reminded her, McCarthy left the room.

Mary continued working, picking the primers from boards and counting them into piles in front of her. She and the other 80 to 100 girls and women in the room had been working for nearly five hours already. Dinner break could not come soon enough. They welcomed a chance to stand, stretch, and relieve their aching backs, necks, and hands. They were seated so closely together on benches that if one person needed to get up to take a privy break, most of the girls on that bench had to get up to let her out. Supervisors discouraged unnecessary disruptions from the work.

Just before the break hour—sometime between 11:00 A.M. and noon—Mary picked up another board. The varnish on this one may have been especially thick. She tried picking the friction primers from the wood, but they wouldn't break free. How many times she tried to lift them off, no one knows. Then she lifted the board and tapped it lightly against the table, hoping to jar the stuck primers loose. She knew this was dangerous, and she had just been warned about it. But nothing happened.

She banged the board a second time, a little harder. Did anyone notice? Still the primers held firm. Frustrated, Mary whacked the board against the table—

BOOM!

Mary Ryan flew into the air and hit the ceiling. As she fell downward—*BOOM!*—a second, much stronger blast filled the entire room. A mass of flames filled the air. Bodies and walls blew apart. The outer walls fell outward, causing the roof to collapse, trapping and smashing dozens of workers. The 50-feet by 20-feet space became a mixture of rubble and humanity.

Screams and moans emerged from the ruins, and some injured workers crawled or ran from the disaster. Not one person in the room escaped unharmed. Many were covered in burns. The only saving grace was that the falling roof had snuffed out most of the fire, so no other rooms or buildings were affected.

Residents along the James River near the island heard the powerful roar, but they weren't alarmed at first. Loud noises were common in that area because of the nearby Tredegar Iron Works factories. The heavy smoke rising from Brown's Island told them that *this* noise, however, accompanied a disaster.

Many in those neighborhoods had relatives—including children—who worked on the island. Swarms of people approached the bridge, maddened by the thought of their loved ones across the span suffering without them. Concerned that a stampede across the bridge would cause it to collapse, the laboratory leaders put sentinels at the mainland entrance to allow only rescue workers onto the island. Hundreds waited long hours as ambulance wagons rolled toward the wreckage. Eventually families were allowed to search for their loved ones as the rescue effort continued.

Between ten and twenty bodies were recovered at first, and they were laid aside. These bodies could not be removed until the coroner examined them, so families of these victims wailed and wept beside them while others continued their search, hoping for a better outcome. Male workers removed debris and uncovered the injured.

The *Richmond Examiner* described what rescuers experienced:

> ... the most heart-rending lamentations issued from the ruins. ... No sooner was one helpless, unrecognizable mass of humanity cared for and removed before the piteous appeals of another would invoke the energy of the rescuers. ... and from twenty to thirty still alive, but suffering the most horrible agonies, blind from burns, with the hair burned from their heads, and the clothing hanging in burning shreds...[2]

Those covered with burns were given a medical treatment that we would consider odd and unsanitary today. After the girls' burnt clothing was removed, their bodies were covered with flour and wrapped in cotton bandages. Then the bandages were saturated with oil. For their pain, the girls were given chloroform, a liquid chemical that was used as an anesthetic. Drops of chloroform were slowly, carefully dripped onto a cloth or sponge placed over a patient's nose and mouth. Breathing in the fumes, the patient fell into a deep and painless sleep.

Just as was the case at the Allegheny Arsenal, many of the victims were so badly burned that they were unrecognizable. A few were identified only by a swatch of fabric or some personal item still attached to the body. Mary Ryan was one of the burn victims. Still alive, she was taken to her father's home on Oregon Hill, about a mile from the island. Other girls ran from the building, their clothing and hair aflame, and didn't stop until they jumped into the river to relieve their suffering. One of those girls, Martha Burley, went under the water but did not come back up.

Many of the dead and injured were crushed under the weight of the fallen roof. Fifteen-year-old Robert Chaple was wedged between a wall and the heavy beams. His skull was crushed, but he was still alive when rescuers found him.

By Saturday evening, a first count showed the extent of the losses: 29 were confirmed dead and at least twice as many were badly hurt. Funerals began on Sunday and continued for the next month as more victims died as a result of their wounds or from related complications. In the end, at least 45 workers—mostly girls and teenagers—perished.[*] Day by day, the newspapers named the casualties as they succumbed to their injuries. Mary Ryan died at home on Monday, March 16. Robert Chaple passed away on

---

An exact count was not possible, as primary-source accounts offered conflicting information.

Wednesday, March 18, and Annie V. Blankenship, 14, died the following day. Almost a month later, on April 10, Martha Burley's body was found in the water. The coroner determined that she had drowned.

A mass grave wasn't necessary to bury the dead from this accident. The victims were buried either at one of the Protestant cemeteries—Hollywood, Shocktoe, or Oakwood—or in the St. Joseph Catholic Cemetery (also called Bishop's) in Richmond. Some have markers with their names, but others lie in unmarked graves in the paupers' section. Sadly, the burial records of the victims in the St. Joseph Cemetery have become lost over time.

Eventually, a memorial for the victims of the C. S. Laboratory explosion was placed at the Oakwood Cemetery, where some 17,000 Confederate soldiers are also buried, making it the second largest Confederate cemetery in the U.S. (See photos on page 76.)

DEATHS CAUSED BY THE C.S. LABORATORY EXPLOSION • MARCH 13, 1863

(Ages are based on 1860 U.S. Census records[‡])

Name (relationship)	Age
Margaret Alexander	15
Mary Archer	12
Emma Virginia Blankenship	14
Mary Blessingham	23
Anne E. Bolton (Boulton)	14
Julia Brannon	22
Maria Brien (Brown)	14
Martha A. Burley	16
Robert S. Chaple	15
Delia Clemens	20
Martha Clemmons	25
James G. Currie	30
Mary Cushing	16
Martha Daley	unknown
Annie Davis	23
Wilhelmina Defenback	15
Ann Dodson	19
Margaret Dustly	16
Sarah Foster	14
Marannie (Mary A.) Garnett	13
Bridget Grimes	14
Sarah Haney	unknown
Nannie Horan (Horin)	14
Barbara A. Jackson	16
Alice Johnson (Johnston)	12
Sarah Marshall	67

Name (relationship)	Age
Virginia A. Mayer	12
Catherine McCarthy	16
Elizabeth S. Moore	15
Adeline Myers	28
Mary O'Brien	16
Mary O'Connors	16
Virginia E. Page	13
Annie Petticord	unknown
Louisa Riceley	unknown
Mary Rowlin	20
Mary Ryan	18
Ella Smith	unknown
Ellen Sullivan	29
Amelia Tiefenback	unknown
Mary E. Valentine	14
Mary Ellen Wallace	12
Mary Whitehurst	15
Eliza Willis	10
Rev. John H. Woodcock	63
Elizabeth Young	33
Mary Zerhum	12
Caroline Zietenheimer	16

‡ *Variations were found in some of the name spellings in 1860 U.S. Census records*

The front (above) and back (below) of the C.S. Laboratory Explosion Memorial in Section G at the Oakwood Cemetery in Richmond, Va.

IN MEMORY OF THOSE WHO LOST THEIR LIVES IN THE EXPLOSION OF C. S. LABORATORIES
ON BROWN'S ISLAND - RICHMOND, VIRGINIA, MARCH 13, 1863

THOUGH THEIR HANDS WERE SMALL AND NOT HARDENED IN BATTLE
THEIR SERVICE TO THE CONFEDERACY LOOMS LARGE
MAY THIS STONE SERVE AS A PERPETUAL MEMORIAL TO THE DEDICATION AND SACRIFICE
OF THESE FORGOTTEN AND UNSUNG VICTIMS

LET US REMEMBER THEM AS TIME AND TIDE MOVE ON IN ENDLESS RHYME
WHILE BUD AND BLOSSOM, HILL AND TREE
REMEMBER THEM SO SHALL WE
OLIVER REEVES

ERECTED BY VIRGINIA DIVISION,
UNITED DAUGHTERS OF THE CONFEDERACY

DEDICATED SEPTEMBER 15, 2001

MARY RYAN, 18
MARY BLESSINGHAM, 12
ELIZA WILLIS, 10
ELIZABETH YOUNG, 33
MARY ARCHER, 12
SARAH HANEY
ANNIE PEDDICORD
MARY ANNIE GARNETT, 13
BARBARA A. JACKSON, 16
ROBERT S. CHAPLE, 15
ELIZABETH S. MOORE, 15
DELIA CLEMENS, 20
SARAH FOSTER, 14
SARAH MARSHALL, 67
REV. JOHN H. WOODCOCK, 63
ALICE JOHNSON, 17
MARY E. VALENTINE, 14
MARGARET DRUSTLY, 16
AMELIA DIEFENBACK, 15
MARY ZERHUM, 12
ANNE E. BOLTON, 14
NANNIE HORAN, 14
VIRGINIA E. PAGE, 13

MARY ELLEN WALLACE, 12
EMMA VIRGINIA BLANKENSHIP, 15
MARGARET ALEXANDER, 15
CAROLINE ZIETENHEIMER, 16
MARTHA CLEMMONS, 25
JAMES CURRIE
MARY O'BRIEN
MARTHA BURLEY
MARTHA DALEY
MRS. ANN DODSON
JULIA A. BRANNON
MARY ROWLIN
CATHERINE MCCARTHY
MARY ZINGINHAM
MARY WHITEHURST
MARIA BRIEN
ELLA SMITH
ANNIE DAVIS
MARY CUSHING
LOUISA RICELY
ELLEN SULLIVAN
MARY O'CONNORS
VIRGINIA A. MAYER, 12

Chapter Five

THE INVESTIGATION & OUTPOURING OF SUPPORT

THE CAUSE OF THE BROWN'S ISLAND EXPLOSION WAS KNOWN THE VERY DAY IT HAPPENED. Even as Mary Ryan was suffering agonizing pain from her burns, she told anyone who would listen that the accident was her fault. She said she hit the primer board and described what happened when it exploded.

Colonel Josiah Gorgas, Chief of Ordnance for the Confederacy, was stunned by the accident. He wrote, "It is terrible to think of—that so much suffering should arise from causes possibly within our control."[3] He also wrote about Mary's admission in his diary:

The accident was caused by the ignition of a friction primer in the hands of a grown girl by the name of Mary Ryan. She. . . gave a clear account of the circumstances. The primer stuck in the varnishing board and she struck

the board three times very hard on the table to drive out the primer. She says she was immediately blown up to the ceiling and on coming down was again blown up.[4]

The colonel could have left it at that and just moved on to quickly rebuild the structure and get back to business. However, his temperament as a conscientious, safety-focused officer led him to initiate a full review of the matter. He chose three men to handle the investigation and to report their findings to him. In less than two weeks, the report was issued.

Besides a moment-by-moment description of the event, based on witnesses' testimonies, the report also looked at the conditions in the room before the accident happened. Although Mary Ryan's act served as the immediate cause of the explosion, the report did not place all of the blame on her young shoulders. The committee reported: "Had this work been going on in a building devoted to that purpose exclusively, the bursting of a primer might have been fatal to the individual handling it but could not have caused such general destruction of life."[5] The extra gunpowder and cartridges in the room that normally would not have been there made this disaster far worse than it should have been.

Captain Wesley N. Smith, the laboratory's superintendent, told the committee that the room held these combustible materials: 200,000 musket caps; 2,000–3,000 friction primers; and 10 or 11 pounds of gunpowder.[6] Gorgas did his duty to the workers by calling for and listening to the investigators' report.

Col. Gorgas used the information to issue new safety regulations for all Confederate arsenals and laboratories. Three of those new rules were:

1) *Friction primers and percussion caps will not be brought into any room that contains loose gunpowder* until *the primers and caps are safely bundled for packing.*

2) *Rooms that have loose powder used for making ammunition will not have more than ten workers at a time.*

3) *As soon as practicable, all workers in these rooms will be given drapes [coverings] made of noncombustible cloth.*[7]

The people of Richmond responded well, too. Even as the first bodies were being taken to their burial sites, community leaders called for donations to aid the victims' families. Outpouring of support was widespread and generous, despite the difficult economy. Soldiers on the battlefield who heard about the disaster sent money to the Richmond newspapers asking them to pass it on to the families with their prayers and condolences. A committee was formed to collect and distribute the gifts that included money, clothing, linens, and other household goods. A benefit ball—common in the South—was organized and held on March 26, 1863. Thousands of dollars were collected over the weeks following that horrific Friday the 13th.

On Brown's Island, a new building went up. On April 4, the *Richmond Examiner* reported: "The Confederates States Laboratory buildings on Brown's Island, destroyed by the explosion, have been replaced or others fitted up, and the work resumed with ample force of female employees, all of whom average from twelve to fifteen dollars a week as the proceeds of their labor."[8]

After all, the women and girls needed jobs, and the war was far from over.

Part III

STARS AND FIRE

at the Washington Arsenal

WASHINGTON, D.C.
JUNE 17, 1864

Chapter Six

GOVERNMENT GIRLS IN THE NATION'S CAPITAL

MORE THAN A YEAR PASSED, AND THE PEOPLE OF BOTH THE CONFEDER-ATE CAPITAL, RICHMOND, AND OF THE U.S. capital, Washington, D.C., were war weary. The monumental cost of lives on both sides continued to grow.

Richmond women were maddened to the point of rebellion against their own leaders during the Bread Riots of 1863. Thousands of women broke into and looted stores. Unable to afford to buy anything with their worthless Confederate currency, the women helped themselves to food, clothing, shoes, and jewelry (which they would use to trade for food). Confederate president Jefferson Davis spoke to the throngs and pleaded with them to settle down. When they refused to disperse, he called out the local militia to quell the disturbance.

Over the rest of 1863 and into the following year, Richmond suffered from more than internal strife. External forces pressed the city, too.

Union General Ulysses S. Grant's men clashed again and again with Confederate General Robert E. Lee's soldiers in the spring of 1864. They fought bloody battles at Spotsylvania, Virginia, and Cold Harbor, just outside Richmond, with both sides suffering great losses. Between May 5 and June 12, the Union Army suffered 50,000 casualties (soldiers killed, mortally wounded, missing, and surviving wounded). Washington filled with bodies as riverboat steamers brought the dead and injured down the Potomac River to the 6th Street wharf. On May 28 alone, more than 3,000 soldiers were taken from the boats to the city's hospitals. Northern newspapers called Grant a "butcher." The general had to find a way to bring this war to an end.

On June 18, Grant's 67,000 men attacked Petersburg, Virginia. Lee had only 20,000. A full day of fighting yielded high losses and few advances for the Union Army. But they held a key position, so General Meade (Union) ordered his men to dig in. It was June 18, 1864, and the siege of Petersburg was beginning. This was the beginning of the end for the Confederate Army.

News of Grant's and Meade's movements came fast and steady into Washington, D.C. Abraham Lincoln was running for re-election, and his attention to any battlefront news was even keener than it had been in the previous years. The unusual heat that settled on the capital two weeks before Independence Day caused additional irritability and impatience. At least the long week was drawing to a close. The success of the siege at Petersburg should have been the biggest news of the weekend. It wasn't.

THE ARSENAL AT GREENLEAF POINT

One of the busiest areas of the capital was the nation's largest federal arsenal. The Washington Arsenal was located at Greenleaf Point, sometimes called "The Island," just south of Washington, D.C., on a peninsula where the Potomac and Anacostia rivers converge. The arsenal was built there in 1810, based on the plans for "Washington City" drawn up by Pierre Charles L'Enfant in 1791. (Today it is Fort Lesley J. McNair.) Greenleaf Point also housed a huge depot that was critical for supplying Union troops with wagons,

Even from the earliest plans for Washington, D.C., this area was set aside as the site of the Washington Arsenal. Today it is the site of Ft. Lesley J. McNair.

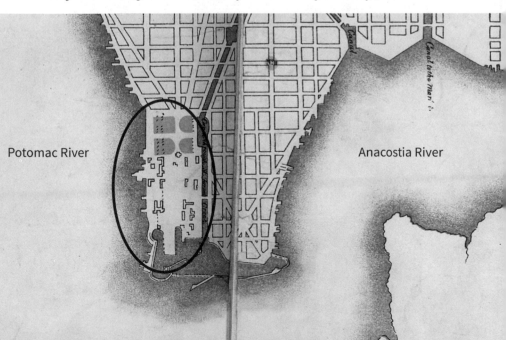

Potomac River

Anacostia River

weapons, and ammunition as they held their places outside Richmond.

Most of the employees at the arsenal were men. They handled the lion's share of the work, especially the heavier work related to artillery: cannons, mortar shells, caissons, limbers, ambulances, and wagons. One of the buildings at the arsenal complex was much like the laboratories at both Allegheny and Richmond. Many of these workers were girls and women, and their main job was making cartridges. In Washington, D.C., women who worked for the government were known as "government girls." Besides arsenal work, some women were hired in the capital to work as clerks at the U.S. Treasury Department and in other government offices.

The girls and women who showed up for work at the arsenal every day were living under the same difficult conditions as the female workers in any arsenal. They were poor, often single, some with disabled parents or husbands, some with husbands at the battlefront, and many with young children to provide for. As in Lawrenceville and Richmond, Irish immigrant girls filled many of these jobs. The women in D.C., however, earned a better wage: between 50 and 60 dollars per month. The cost of living in the capital, even in the poor neighborhoods near the arsenal, was high, and half or more of their income paid for rent alone. Their wages kept them housed and fed, but not much more.

Still, arsenal work was more honorable than the other prevalent option for young women in Washington. Uneducated immigrant girls often had to resort to prostitution

GOVERNMENT GIRLS AT WORK

One of the entry-level jobs available in Washington was as a clerk at the U.S. Treasury Department. Young men held these positions until the Civil War began. Many of them volunteered to serve, so U.S. Treasurer Francis E. Spinner, who believed the boys were of better use as soldiers, decided to replace them with young women. The girls were involved in three tasks at the Treasury Department. First, currency trimmers used scissors to cut apart individual greenbacks that had been printed on a sheet of paper, usually four per sheet. Second, others counted currency, keeping a lookout for torn, defaced, and counterfeit bills. Third, girls with excellent penmanship became copyists who hand-wrote signatures on the currency. All of them worked 10- or 12-hour days. The salary for these jobs was $600 per year, half what the young men before them had been paid.

Government girls also worked at the War Department, the U.S. Patent Office, the U.S. Mint, and the post office. Societal pressure made the government provide separate workspaces for women, because many felt it was "improper" for women to work alongside men.

After the war was over, girls and women continued to work for the U.S. government, and in 1870, Congress passed a law granting equal pay to women who worked as clerks. They were seldom promoted to better-paying jobs, however.

A Harper's Weekly sketch from 1865 shows female clerks leaving work at the U.S. Treasury Department.

to earn a living. The city was particularly infamous for its brothels, where a new girl was always welcome.

The bustling city seemed never to sleep. Carriages of all kinds rolled over the cobblestone streets, taking men to their businesses or to meetings and women to shops or gatherings where gossip and tea were mixed with honey. Of course, these were the upper-class residents and visitors. Others, including the girls at the U.S. Treasury and at the Washington Arsenal, put on their plain dresses, hooped skirts and all, and walked to their workplaces.

The girls walked south down 4 ½ Street to enter the arsenal area. The place looked like a park—except for the pyramids of stacked cannonballs and the large artillery pieces on the grounds. More than 40 buildings made up the Washington Arsenal. They included laboratories, storehouses, icehouses, carpentry and paint shops, tool sheds, stables, blacksmith shops, a bakery, a hospital, a commissary, and living quarters for officers and enlisted men. The building nearest the entrance was a large, impressive brick structure that had once housed the federal penitentiary. (It was used as a prison again, a year later, when four of the people linked to Lincoln's assassination were held, tried, and hanged there in July 1865. Later, John Wilkes Booth's body was brought there, too, and buried in a cellar until his family came for his remains.)

The girls could not help but be impressed by the complex, especially when compared to the section of town where they lived. Thousands of families found a home in the Island's residential area. Side by side, shacks and boarding houses became homes for workers at nearby wharfs, railroads, and marketplaces. These were working-class people: laborers, rivermen, wagonners, seamstresses, and servants. Within those low-rent houses lived native-born Americans, immigrants, free blacks, and poor whites.

Their rent didn't get them much. The entire area had no sidewalks, and worse, no sewers. Sanitation was horrible, and a multitude of pests lived there, too: flies, mosquitoes, roaches, and fleas. The capital city, a few blocks north, struggled with the same sanitation problems. The Island residents may have been poor, but they were hard-working and compassionate people. They often came together during hard times and helped families in desperate need.

The girls tried to disregard the heat as they headed toward the five-room laboratory building where more than 100 of them worked. The one-story structure was made of wood on three sides, and the back wall was brick. Overhead was a metal roof. The five rooms were separated by the kind of work being done. At one end was the cylinder room. In the center were the box room, the office, and the choking room. In the other end, workers were busy choking and packing cartridges.

Kate Horan felt the oppressive heat on Friday, June 17, but she also carried the normal daily sadness of leaving her four children: John, age 6; William, age 4; Joseph, age 2; and infant daughter, Mary. Kate was only 25 years old, but so much depended on her. She reminded herself of this every day when she looked at their little faces. Other girls and women were helping their widowed mothers by bringing in extra money. Some, like Sallie McElfresh, were only 12 years old. Kate, Sallie, and the others female workers made cartridges. They turned paper, gunpowder, and minié balls into lethal ammunition for the Union Army. No doubt the cartridges they had made just days or weeks ago were now with the boys in Petersburg, Virginia.

Superintendent Tom Brown, age 47, had other things on his mind that day. The 4th of July was around the corner, and he needed to fill large orders for red and white "stars," or flares, that the officers on the battlefield wanted so they could celebrate Independence Day with their boys. (The South did not celebrate Independence Day at all.) At any other time of year, the flares were not as high in demand because they were only used to illuminate an area during a night battle.

Brown called himself a pyrotechnist, even though he had no formal scientific training. Still, explosives were his specialty. Over the 23 years he had been working at the arsenal, Brown mixed powders and chemicals to make a variety of explosives. The Ordnance Department had a manual with specific formulas for each product, but Brown liked to play with the "recipes." He felt he was making the mixtures safer than the ones the Ordnance Department recommended.

Brown was glad for the heat that day. Over the previous two weeks, daytime high temperatures had sometimes reached more than 100°F. His "stars" needed heat in order to dry. Brown mixed three ingredients—potassium chloride, strontium nitrate, and carbon—and formed them into gumball-sized nuggets. They were wet when first mixed, so he had devised a way to dry them, a method he had been using for a long time. He had three deep copper pans that had been painted black, because black absorbs heat. Brown placed 200 to 300 wet "stars" into each pan. Then he carried the pans outside to an area under some trees where no one usually walked, a place near the center of the arsenal compound where three buildings stood. He believed this was safe because it was unlikely anyone would jostle the pans and cause them to explode.

One of those nearby buildings was the laboratory where more than 100 women and girls worked—the building where Kate Horan and Sallie McElfresh worked.

Famous photographer Mathew Brady took this picture sometime in early June 1864, showing the building at the Washington Arsenal where the women worked. Some, if not all, of the women in this photo became victims of the explosion on June 17, 1864.

Chapter Seven

A CAPITAL DISASTER

THE FEMALE WORKERS IN THE LABORATORY HAD SPECIFIC TASKS TO COMPLETE. About 80 of them divided their time between making paper cylinders and packing finished cartridges. Another 30 filled the cylinders with gunpowder and minié balls, and then choked them closed with string. Three boys were assigned to the building to sweep up loose gunpowder and move boxes from one room to another.

The boys were free to come and go, but the girls had to stay seated on their benches unless they asked permission to be excused. Then all of the girls on that bench would stand, move, and let the woman out. The same had to happen when she returned. They worked from 6:00 A.M. to 6:00 P.M., six days a week, and got two one-hour breaks for breakfast and dinner (lunch).

The office for all of the laboratories was in the center

of this building. Four men worked at their desks and were able to constantly monitor the workers in the rooms around them. These men were Tom Brown, superintendent; Brown's assistant, Andrew Cox; chief clerk Hosea Moulton; and Major E. N. Stebbins, the storekeeper in charge of inventory.

The men and women at the Washington Arsenal knew the work was dangerous. Everyone there had heard about the catastrophes at other arsenals, too. They knew about the Allegheny Arsenal and the C.S. Laboratory explosions. They also heard about smaller incidents in Jackson, Mississippi; Philadelphia, Pennsylvania; and Waterbury, Connecticut. In fact, that very morning, one of their supervisors had read a thank-you letter to the girls in the room. It was in response to the donation the workers from the Washington Arsenal had sent to the Allegheny Arsenal victims' families: $170 to help them pay for a monument so their loved ones would be remembered. After hearing the letter read to them, the girls went back to work.

The windows in the building were set high, and even though they were open, whatever breeze came through did little to cool the air. The ladies had nothing to use as a fan, because that might cause the gunpowder near them to blow away. They weren't allowed to talk, either, although singing was encouraged. They noticed that one of the girls wasn't in her spot, and rumors had swirled on the way into work that she had been fired for being too chatty.

By noon, the temperature neared 90°F. This might be

another 100-degree-day. Superintendent Brown's drying stars had been in the sun for more than two hours, and they were long-past dry. In the alcove where he placed them, they sat getting hotter and hotter.

South of the laboratory in the carriage shop, 18-year-old Thomas Clinton was looking outside and saw something explode. A streaming flare colored the sky with red and white sparks. From his vantage point, Thomas could see the outside of the back wall of the choking room. He didn't think much about it and assumed Brown was setting off fireworks. Inside the choking room of the building, Henry Seufferle, 16, was sweeping when he saw a spark fly through one of the high windows in the back and fall into the room. He dropped his broom and ran, yelling a warning.

At the same moment, Major Stebbins saw something out of the corner of his eye and went outside the office to look. Mr. Cox, also in the office, saw a flash and tried to run. Stebbins was starting to enter the choking room.

It was 11:50 A.M.

The explosion thundered, and a flash of light as bright as lightning filled the room. A river of flames headed toward the boxes of cartridges on the table. The blast blew the door to the room shut. Stebbins quickly opened the door, and as more oxygen filled the air, another explosion erupted. The roof blew straight up and came crashing down on the fire-filled space. Experts estimated that the room may have reached 3000°F during the blast. (Even modern crematoriums seldom exceed 1800°F to turn bodies into ashes.)

The girls who sat on the bench against the back wall never had a chance to move. Others tried to run to the door or toward the windows. Those whose dresses were on fire didn't realize that they were spreading the flames when their wide skirts touched the fabric of other girls' dresses. Hot lead from the minié balls melted into the cloth and skin of the victims.

Kate Palmer climbed up and jumped out a window, only to impale her neck on a piece of metal on the other side. But she survived.

Catherine Goldsmith was covered with burns and was scarred for life. But she survived.

Most of the girls and women never made it out of the room.

Superintendent Brown was forced out of his office by the explosion, but was unharmed.

All of the male workers on the compound rushed toward the burning building. They saw thick, black smoke rising from the high windows, darkening the noonday sun. Women were crawling out of those windows; some fell and broke bones as they landed. As the men encountered girls who looked like running fireballs, they threw large tarps on them or tore flaming clothes away from their skin. Some men carried girls, still on fire, to the river to extinguish the flames, often getting serious burns on their hands and upper bodies as a result. Hosea Moulton, who had been in the office when the explosion occurred, went into the room and carried out one of the girls, getting severely burned in the process. Major Stebbins helped rescue 30 workers, but many of the survivors rescued themselves. Some of the injured girls fled the area and didn't stop until they reached their homes.

Fire companies from the arsenal arrived quickly. They put out the flames and watered down any adjoining areas to prevent the fire from spreading. By 1:15 P.M., the conflagration was completely extinguished.

By then, families were lining up at the arsenal's entrance. They may or may not have heard the explosion, but they certainly could see the columns of smoke rising from the area. The Veteran Reserve Corps was called in to secure the gates, only allowing entry to essential personnel. The families would have to wait.

While the injured were being attended to and readied for transportation to a hospital or to their homes, the coroner was doing his job. The dead had to be identified and causes of death determined.

Workers went through the ruins to recover bodies. As they were found, the victims were placed upon boards and carried outside the building. A large tarp covered the group. Soon only body parts and items that might help identify victims were removed. They were placed in boxes and small pans and placed beside the burned bodies under the tarp. The *Daily National Intelligencer* newspaper reported the "a half dozen of the bodies were put in a box about five feet square."[1]

Seventeen bodies were found. Some of them still had the metal hoops of their crinolines encircling them. Relatives would be horrified by what remained of their loved ones. The Washington, D.C. *Evening Star* reported about the scene:

> The charred remains of seventeen dead bodies lay scattered about, some in boxes, some on pieces of boards, and some in large tin pans, they having been removed from the ruins in these receptacles. In nearly every case, only the trunk of the body remained, the arms and legs being missing or detached. In one case, however, that of a young girl, every shred of dress had been burned from her but her gaiter shoes, which had singularly escaped a touch of the flames....
>
> A singular feature of the sad spectacle was that presented by a number of the bodies nearly burned to a cinder being caged, as it were, in the wire of their hooped skirts....
>
> Many of the bodies seemed to have been crisped quite bloodless, the flesh, where exposed, being perfectly white...."[2]

Johanna Connor was 20 years old. The only identifiable item on her body was a piece of cloth and a belt. The top of her head was missing. Someone wrote, "This is Johanna O'Conner" [sic] on a note and placed it by her skull.

Other victims' bodies could only be identified by clothing or a piece of jewelry or a shoe. Bridget Dunn was identified only because she was "of large size."

Some of the names on the list of the dead were added only because they had been at work but afterward were missing, and there was even some confusion about that because the office books were destroyed in the fire. No identifiable body part or piece of clothing was found for them. Emma Arnold Tippett was one of these women. In the 1860 U.S. Census, Emma was listed as single and 19 years old. Four years later, she was married and had an infant, whom her mother, Anna, cared for. When Emma's mother came looking for her daughter's body, she fainted at the sight of the mass of burned, unknowable humanity. When she went home to her grandbaby, Anna was met by the news that Emma's husband had just died at an army hospital.

After the explosion and rescue of the victims, only the brick wall of the building, shown here, remained standing.

DEATHS CAUSED BY THE WASHINGTON ARSENAL EXPLOSION OF JUNE 17, 1864

(Ages are based on 1860 U.S. Census records.)

Name	Age
Melissa Adams*	18
Annie Bache	10
Emma Baird*	23
Lizzie Brahler‡	13
Bettie Branagam‡	unknown
Kate Brosnaham*	unknown
Mary Burroughs*	22
Emily Collins‡	13
Johanna Connor	20
Bridget Dunn	unknown
Susan Harris*	19
Kate Horan	25
Rebecca Hull	40

Name	Age
Eliza Lacey‡	unknown
Louisa (Lizzie) Lloyd*	unknown
Sallie McElfresh	12
Julie McEwen‡	21
Ellen Roche*	18
Pinkey Scott	unknown
Mrs. W.E. (Emma) Tippett*	23
Margaret Yonson‡	unknown

indicates body was unidentifiable

‡ *indicates body was left at the arsenal rather than taken home for burial*

Chapter Eight

AN IMMEDIATE INVESTIGATION

As soon as Secretary of War Edwin Stanton heard about the explosion, he ordered an immediate and thorough investigation as to the cause. He created a three-man board to conduct the inquiry. Major General Silas Casey was to lead the team, so the group was known as the "Casey Board." They began their work the afternoon of the incident.

The men walked through the laboratory area, looked at the wreckage, and interviewed only four men: Commandant of the arsenal Major James Benton; Superintendent Thomas Brown; Andrew Cox, assistant to the superintendent; and paymaster and storekeeper Major E. N. Stebbins. The board learned that 104 workers had been working in the building that day: 25 in the choking room where the fire occurred, and 79 in other areas of the building. The testimony from each man was straightforward and clear. Some stars were left to dry in the sun opposite the south-facing windows of the choking room. They spontaneously caught fire, causing one to enter one of the windows in the room.

The Casey Board didn't need to hear any more. A three-page report described their findings. The group wrote in the report that "a part of one [of the stars was] drawn into the nearest open window of the choking room, lodged among the cartridges, a box of which was placed in front of each operator, and set them on fire. Almost instantaneously the fire was communicated to the other boxes and hence, the explosion. The fire spread rapidly and soon the entire building was in flames."[3]

Cause: The explosion and subsequent fire were started by "rocket stars" drying nearby. This was a rare accident that "would scarcely ever occur again."[4]

Recommendation: Combustible material should not be dried near areas where munitions are made.

The Casey Board did not blame or hold anyone accountable for the explosion.

THE CORONER'S INQUEST

That was not the end of interrogations. The city's coroner arrived at the scene around 4:00 P.M. Before doing anything else, he formed a 12-member jury of inquest made up of male arsenal workers. Their first task was difficult. With the coroner, the group viewed all of the victims' remains. The coroner took careful notes and talked to the people who helped identify the dead. He released the bodies of Johanna

Connor, Rebecca Hull, and Bridget Dunn to their families. They were carried home in straw-filled boxes. Eight were burned beyond recognition, and so little was left of them that their families had nothing to take home. Several bodies were left at the scene. Perhaps there were no family members to come for them or the families were too poor to manage their burials. There is no way to know.

Then came the interviews. The coroner talked with the same four men who had been questioned by the Casey Board, but they also interviewed two boys, Thomas Clinton and Henry Seufferle. The 12 jurors listened carefully as details about the disaster unfolded.

Superintendent Brown told the coroner that he had placed the stars out to dry. He put them where he had always put them, and he testified that his own mixture of materials was actually safer than stars made using the Ordnance Department's manual. He told the men that he could not say for certain that his stars caused the fire.

Commandant Benton had not been near the laboratory when the fire began. He told the board that his primary focus was to get the fire out so it would not spread to other buildings. While working with the men, he had found the pans. He said they were covered with white residue and were most likely the cause of the explosion. He told the men that he had stressed safety to Brown, but he also felt that the superintendent was a competent person. Regardless, Benton felt it was "imprudent" for him to have left so many of the stars out to dry at once.[5] Defending Brown, the commandant said he believed this was an oversight on Brown's part and was not in any way intentional.

Benton's testimony regarding the workers was helpful, but disturbing. He explained what their work was, making cartridges, and that finished cartridges were placed in boxes—directly in front of the girls—on the tables. The bullet top (minié ball) of each cartridge was pointed toward the workers. He said, ". . . at the time of the explosion more or less injury was done to the girls by their being struck by these balls as the cartridges exploded."[6]

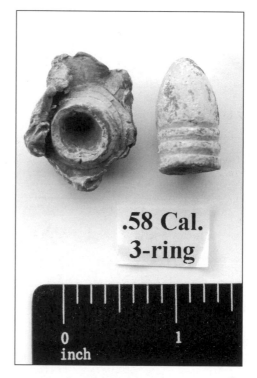

On the right, a minié ball before use. The bullet on the left has been fired and hit something soft, like human tissue. The lead bullet did a lot of damage and usually stayed embedded in its victim.

Andrew Cox, Brown's assistant, told the board that he also saw the pans, and he thought there were between 800 and 900 stars altogether. He tried to make a list of the workers in the room, but all of the records in the office burned in the fire. He estimated that there were about 30 women, but could recall only 25 names. The attendance records had burned along with everything else in the building.

Major Stebbins provided the most descriptive and damaging (to Brown) account. He said he saw something flying outside the southern windows of the building and walked out of the office to get a better look. Once outside, he saw "stars flying about."[7] Some were launched 40 feet, toward the river. He returned to tell Brown and Cox what he saw when the explosion happened, blowing the doors shut. He opened them, and as he entered the room, two cartridge boxes exploded. However, he recalled seeing no loose gunpowder beyond what was normal. The small amount that was on the tables was enough to ignite and spread the fire like a flash down the table, blinding the girls and setting their clothes on fire. He saw them running, trying to escape. As they ran, they brushed against others and set each other on fire. He believed that all of the girls on the south side of the table died at their seats. Finally, he told the board that he helped about 40 women out of the building and used tarps to cover those whose clothing was aflame.

Henry Seufferle, one of the sweepers free to roam around the outside, said he saw three copper pans behind the building. He recalled there was between 200 and 300 stars in each. While he was in the choking room sweeping, he saw a flare coming through the window on the southern side of the building and ran outside. Seufferle helped two girls safely off the porch and watched as the men rescued workers, getting them outside to safety.

Thomas Clinton testified that he saw some fireworks from a distance and figured Brown was setting them off. Then he saw the building erupt into a huge blaze.

The coroner heard all he needed to do his job. He determined the same cause of death for each of the victims.

> **That the body of a female came to her death by the explosion of the laboratory of the Washington Arsenal, where she was employed choking cartridges; that the said explosion took place about ten minutes to 12 n., and it was caused by the superintendent, Thomas B. Brown, placing three metallic pans some thirty feet from the laboratory, containing chemical preparations intended for the manufacture of white and red stars; that the sun's rays operating on the metallic pans caused spontaneous combustion, scattering the fire in every direction, a portion flying into the choking room . . .** [8]

Although the military investigation placed no blame on Brown, the coroner's jury did. In plain language, they stated he was "guilty of the most culpable carelessness and negligence in placing highly combustible substances so near a building filled with human beings, indicating a most reckless disregard for life, which should be severely rebuked by the Government."[9]

There is no evidence that Brown was reprimanded for his part in this disaster. No one called for charges to be drawn up against him, but local newspapers did suggest Brown should not be allowed to work where such an incident could happen again. Within a year, Andrew Cox replaced Brown as the arsenal's superintendent. Unbelievably, Brown continued to work at the arsenal as its pyrotechnist for at least the next decade, despite two more explosions that killed nine men and destroyed several buildings.

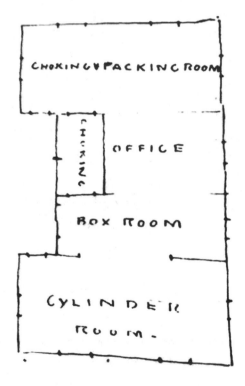

Sketch of the laboratory building at Washington Arsenal

Chapter Nine

OF DEATH AND DECORUM

THE SHADOWS OF NIGHT FINALLY COVERED THE SCENE AS FAMILIES LEFT. Male arsenal workers stayed on to attend to the fourteen bodies left behind under the large tarps. Some of the men wrapped the remains in cloth and placed them in individual boxes. The boxes were carried to the carpentry shop where a night guard stood watch. Commandant Benton had received a telegram from Secretary Stanton telling him that all of the funeral expenses for the victims would be paid by the War Department. It was up to the arsenal to make sure every girl received a suitable burial.

Work was called off for all arsenal workers the next day, but that did not mean they didn't show up and get busy. Carpenters and their helpers began the work of making coffins. These men were craftsmen, and they chose the best materials to help honor the girls' memories. The coffins were made of poplar wood and stained a rich, dark brown. They were lined with muslin and white satin. The handles and nameplates were silver-plated. The names of the girls who had been identified were engraved on the nameplate; eight simply read, "Unknown."

Saturday's newspapers reported that two more girls had died overnight: 12-year-old Sallie McElfresh and 17-year-old Annie Bache.

Different groups were formed to handle the multitude of details for the funeral and after. Some men formed a committee to collect money as relief funds for families of the deceased and injured. By a unanimous vote, the arsenal workers agreed to each donate a full day's pay to help them. Three men chose a gravesite at the Congressional Cemetery as a resting place for most of the girls. Some families were making their own arrangements at other cemeteries. Three other men were assigned to get hearses and pallbearers and to make decisions about the funeral service itself, scheduled for 3:00 P.M. on Sunday. Others talked with the families to arrange for their attendance at the funeral. Most of these families had no resources to count on and certainly no carriages for riding in a funeral procession. Thanks to these workers and the offer by the War Department, every detail was taken care of. Before Saturday had ended, the workers agreed to meet again on Monday to discuss having a fundraiser to erect a monument at the gravesite "to the memory of those who lost their lives in the Government employment."[10]

AN UNMATCHED FUNERAL PROCESSION

Local newspapers, most notably the *National Republican* and the *Evening Star*, provided stunning descriptions of the funeral on Sunday, June 19. Never before had such a funeral taken place in the capital for someone who was not a dignitary. Readers were moved as they read Monday's lengthy newspaper accounts.

The funeral was set to begin at 3:00 P.M. at the rear of one of the storehouses near the front of the compound. (It would have been dangerous to let people just mill about on the arsenal grounds.) Despite the heat—it was going to be another hot, dry day—nearly 1,000 people flocked to the arsenal three hours early. They were stopped at the gate and waited there until 2:30. By then, several thousand people had arrived, and they pushed through the gate.

A large canopy covered a platform, fifteen by twenty feet. The canopy was draped with an American flag and black mourning rosettes. In the center of the platform were two rows of coffins. In one row, seven coffins were lined up, and on each was a girl's name: Annie Bache, Julia McEwen, Emily Collins, Elizabeth Branagan, Lizzie Brahler, Eliza Lacey, and Maggie Yonson. In the other row, eight coffins each bore a nameplate that simply read "Unknown." Every coffin was adorned with flowers—white lilies and roses, as befitting young ladies—provided as a tribute by their fellow female workers at the arsenal. Family members were allowed to go onto the platform to say their final goodbyes.

LINCOLN'S OWN GRIEF

Abraham Lincoln was well acquainted with loss. His beloved mother, Nancy, died an agonizing death from "milk sickness" at age 34. He was just nine years old. His older sister, Sarah, became like a mother to him. When she was only 20 years old, Sarah Lincoln Grigsby died after delivering a stillborn baby boy. Lincoln blamed her husband for refusing to call a doctor to help his sister.

While Lincoln was in the state legislature and lived in New Salem, Illinois, he became good friends with the Rutledge family, and was especially fond of their daughter, Anne. In August 1835, at the tender age of 22, Anne contracted what was probably typhoid fever. He visited her almost daily until her death on August 25th. His friends shared concern about the depth of grief, even depression, which Lincoln carried with him for a long time afterward. The deaths of these young women deeply affected Lincoln.

The 1840s and 50s brought Lincoln marriage to Mary Todd, political success, and the birth of his four sons: Robert, Eddy, Willie, and Tad. Surviving to adulthood was not an easy thing for children in the nineteenth century. In 1850, when not quite four years old, Eddy died of what the U.S. census listed as "chronic consumption." He lay ill for 52 days before passing away at home in Springfield, Illinois. Abraham and Mary were bereft with grief. Leaving Springfield for Washington, D.C., when Lincoln was elected president was difficult for the parents, especially for Mary, because they had to leave the place where little Eddy was buried.

While living at the White House, Lincoln's two youngest sons fell victim to an epidemic of typhoid fever. Willie, age 11, and Tad, age 8, were attended to by the best doctors in Washington, but Willie did not survive. He died on February 20, 1862. The funeral procession for Willie was lengthy, like the one for the arsenal victims. Two white horses pulled the hearse, followed by two black horses of the Lincolns' carriage. Mary Lincoln never fully recovered from this loss. President Lincoln grieved openly at first, then went about his work trying to save the Union—but he regularly visited Willie's grave at the Oak Hill Cemetery.

The heavy loss of life during the war weighed on him, too. On June 16, 1864 (just one day before the tragic explosion at the arsenal), Lincoln expressed the sadness he carried about the war:

War, at its best, is terrible, and this war of ours, in its magnitude and in its duration, is one of the most terrible. It has deranged business, totally in many localities, and partially in all localities. It has destroyed property, and ruined homes; it has produced a national debt and taxation unprecedented, at least in this country. It has carried mourning to almost every home, until it can almost be said that the 'heavens are hung in black.' [11]

It is fitting that Lincoln would be a "Chief Mourner" at the funeral for the victims of the Washington Arsenal disaster. When he led the procession to the cemetery and bowed his head during heartfelt prayers for the dead girls, Lincoln represented both the nation and himself as President and as someone who understood personal loss.

Photographs taken in 1861 (left) and 1865 show how Lincoln aged during his presidency.

Some became hysterical when they found their loved one's name. Others kept looking, only to be disappointed when their daughter's or sister's name could not be found. Their girl was one of the "unknown."

Local ministers and priests spoke and prayed, reminding the living of the fragility of life and the need to be ready to meet God when their time on Earth was over. Then the Chief Marshal of the ceremony invited families and friends of the deceased to get into their carriages and follow the hearses to the cemetery. The procession left the north gate of the arsenal around 4:00 P.M.

A band led the long line of mourners, which was followed by the official clergyman, the hearses, and the Chief Mourners: President Abraham Lincoln and Secretary Stanton. Then came the officers of the arsenal and the relatives and friends of the victims. A good number of arsenal employees and members of the community brought up the rear. The procession was about three miles long and took more than half an hour to pass any given point. The *Evening Star* reported about 150 rented carriages (called "hacks") besides the other vehicles and many people on horseback. Most of the attendees walked.

When the procession reached the crossroads of 4½ Street and F Street, everyone stopped to allow another hearse join the line. In it was the body of Sallie McElfresh. As the funeral line moved on, bystanders crowded the street edges, paying their respects to the dead. The closer the procession got to the cemetery on Pennsylvania Avenue, the larger the crowds grew. Hours before, many had already taken a place at the burial site.

Two of the hearses separated from the line and moved to other sites. Sallie McElfresh would be buried near her father, who had recently died of typhoid, and four infant siblings who had died between 1857 and 1860. Annie Bache was laid to rest in her family's vault. Four funerals had already taken place on Saturday at Mount Olivet, the Catholic cemetery. They were for Bridget Dunn, Kate Horan, Catherine Hull, and Johanna Connor.

The procession stopped on the west side of Congressional Cemetery. Two large holes had been dug, each one fifteen feet wide, six feet long, and nearly six feet deep. Six feet of untouched grass lay between them. One by one, each of the coffins with names on them was lowered into one pit. In the same manner, the coffins of the "unknown" were placed in the other.

The *Evening Star* ended its description with these words:

"No such demonstrations of popular sympathy has ever been expressed in Washington before as by this immense out-pouring of people to attend the funeral of the victims of this sad disaster, and the demonstration will long be remembered by those who witnessed it."[12]

THE MONUMENT THAT STILL STANDS

The workers at the Washington Arsenal began work immediately on a monument. At 12:30 P.M. on Monday, the day after the funeral, they met to discuss how to raise money for the project. They made a circular (similar to an advertisement) to be run in the local newspapers asking for proposals for the building of the monument. The notice also explained how people, businesses, and organizations could make contributions to help pay for it—and to be wary of unscrupulous people who might take advantage by asking for donations for the cause but never intended to part with that money.

On the Fourth of July, two things happened that were related to the arsenal disaster. First, the U.S. Congress passed a "Joint Resolution for the Relief of the Sufferers by a Late Accident at the U.S. Arsenal in Washington, D.C." Explaining that the survivors were poor and had depended on the victims' earnings to live, the Congress stated that:

> . . . the sum of two thousand dollars be, and the same is hereby, appropriated out of any money in the treasury not otherwise appropriated, for the relief of the victims of such explosion—said money to be distributed under the direction of Major Benton, commanding at said arsenal, and in such manner as shall most conduce to the comfort and relief of said sufferers, according to their necessities respectively, and that he report to this house.[13]

Major Benton accounted for every penny. Some of the money went to help pay for victims' medicine, and a little more than half of the total was paid to 110 women, or their survivors, to replace the clothes that were damaged by the fire. With the exception of monies given to the orphaned children of the dead, however, none of the two thousand dollars was given to the families of the deceased for their loss of income.

The second event on this day was more directly related to the disaster. One more woman was added to the list of the dead. Pinkey Scott, a young widow, was the last of the women to die from her injuries. She left behind two orphaned children. Her name would join the 20 others on the proposed monument.

Soon monument committee had collected $3,000. After reviewing designs from 19 companies, the committee chose the Flannery Brothers of Washington, D.C., to build the structure. A year after the arsenal explosion, a beautiful memorial was dedicated as it stood over the cluster of graves at the Congressional Cemetery. On the top is a life-sized figure named "Grief," a young woman looking down upon the buried girls.

The front panel on the pedestal shows a building with smoke pouring from its windows, and beneath the image it reads:

Killed

By An Explosion

At The U.S. Arsenal
Washington, D.C.
June 17th 1864

The back panel is inscribed:
Erected
By Public Contributions
By the Citizens Of
Washington, D.C.
June 17th 1865

The east- and west-facing sides list the names of the victims. Twenty-one more women and girls had become casualties of a war that draped a veil of death over thousands of homes and our entire nation.

EPILOGUE

Almost another year would pass before the war ended. At arsenals in the North and South, girls and women continued to produce the ammunition soldiers needed to keep fighting. Not much changed in those months. The job was still dangerous. The girls still needed to work. No one was ever held responsible in any real way for the deaths of all those workers in Lawrenceville, Richmond, and Washington.

The women at the Watertown Arsenal in Massachusetts did not remain silent about the issues at their workplace. They knew *they* could become the next tragedy, so the ladies got together, wrote, and signed a petition about the working conditions in their arsenal. First, they petitioned their arsenal superintendent, Colonel Rodman, about their concerns. Nothing happened. Then they petitioned their congressman, Daniel Gooch, who just happened to be a member of the Committee on the Conduct of War.

These Watertown women were smart. They knew their grievances had to go beyond their concern for their own safety. That wasn't enough to get anyone to act—or to care. Their carefully worded petition used political innuendo to achieve their goal. Could it be that Colonel Rodman and the women's supervisor, Major Hilton, were pro-Confederate sympathizers? Gooch, a Republican, saw an opportunity to investigate the leaders of the Watertown Arsenal. The investigation quickly turned from the women's safety concerns—careless experiments with gunpowder in highly volatile areas—to the arsenal's political agendas and reports of inappropriate sexual activities at the arsenal. Once again, the workers' safety and other job-related concerns were swept under the rug, like gunpowder dust.

The war ended in April 1865. Some of the arsenal girls and women went back home, but others continued to work. Their husbands and fathers may have come back from the war too injured to be able to work. Many did not return at all.

Employment of women and children increased as the industrialization of American grew, but their working conditions did not improve. Decades passed before adequate laws addressed and protected these vulnerable workers. If you'd like to know more about the U.S. labor reform movement, you can investigate this important part of American history. I have chosen a list of books to get you started in the Recommended Reading section.

Author's Note

I BEGAN WRITING AN ENTIRELY DIFFERENT BOOK. I researched a topic that was wider—and safer. Taking a look at the various roles women held during the Civil War, I discovered nurses, Sanitary Commission organizers, and even some soldiers and spies who were women. Thousands of women organized efforts that became the homefront aid machines, producing amazing amounts of materials that were desperately needed to keep soldiers fed, clothed, and medically cared for. Northern and Southern women raised hundreds of thousands of dollars for the war. Many took up the cause of nursing the wounded. But none of them spoke to me. They all had been written about before.

I studied groups of women whose lives were disrupted when their men rode off to volunteer as soldiers. I could almost see them standing at their open doors, watching husbands and sons grow smaller as they headed toward the battlefield and an unknowable future. I imagined how hard it would have been to close that door. Most of these women endured. Some even thrived as they stepped into power they'd never been given before. They managed their households, their finances, and their lives on their terms now.

As I was reading about these women, I discovered another group, barely mentioned in most accounts. Some of these women were so young they could only be called children. While other women were busy making and gathering goods from their homes, these girls left their houses every day to sit quietly, face-forward, at tables covered with gunpowder and lead in U.S. and Confederate arsenals.

Few books mentioned these girls, so I began to dig. I typed the keywords "Civil War women arsenal workers" into the Google search bar. There, on the internet, I found what I couldn't find in books. Articles from newspapers and magazines written by people in Pittsburgh, Richmond, and Washington, D.C., gave me details, primary source links, and—best of all—names. I wanted to know these girls. I began searching for their names like I was searching for loved ones in an overgrown cemetery. I knew this was the book that had to be written.

Armed with those names, I could look deeper, go farther back in time. The U.S. Census records offered an astonishing amount of information. I've done a lot of family research (genealogy) online, and filled branches and branches of my own family tree. As I put in every single name of the victims of these disasters, I felt as if I was looking for family. I focused on the 1860 census, the one just before the time when they died. Some names never appeared in the searches. I tried every variation I could think of to find them. They lay hidden. Thankfully, many other searches yielded results. For example, I typed in "Elizabeth Alger," birth year approximately 1842, lived in Allegheny County, Pennsylvania, female. I hit Enter. There she was!

"Elizebeth Alger" (the spelling on other lists had been Anglicized)

"Age 18" (in 1860) "Born in Pennsylvania"

"Father, Joseph, age 66, illiterate, born in Germany, laborer

"Mother, Elizebeth, age 55, illiterate, born in Germany, washerwoman"

(I wondered: *Were they really illiterate or did they just not speak English?*)

She had three sisters: Mary, 22, Margaret, 10, and Matilda, 8. (*Did Mary also work at the arsenal, but survived?*)

None of them could know that in two years, Elizebeth would die in the Allegheny Arsenal explosion.

Each girl and woman became someone I wanted to know—as much as I could, more than 150 years later. Basic information on a flat sheet of paper gave me more than I expected. Details became circumstances, and circumstances bred empathy. The urge to tell their stories kept me awake at night. The need to make sure these victims would not be forgotten became the energy that created the book you're now holding.

Now you know them, too. Now you can tell others about these poor immigrant girls, these hard-working daughters and mothers. They deserve to be remembered because they represent so many others like them who worked in unsafe workplaces, who struggled to earn a basic living, and who believed that hard work was better than handouts.

Today you can visit memorials in three cemeteries, markers that list their names and tell the reason for so much death. At the Allegheny Cemetery, in Pittsburgh, Pennsylvania, a simple marble and bronze monument replaces the eroded memorial that had been set up in 1863. It lists all of the victims' names and stands above the mass grave where 45 of the 78 bodies lie. In Richmond, Virginia, only recently, in 2001, was a memorial erected to commemorate the lives lost in the C.S. Laboratory explosion. It is in the Oakwood Cemetery there. Only at the Congressional Cemetery in Washington, D.C, will you find a true monument, one that shows and tells the story of the girls who came to work one day but never walked home again.

Words from the Allegheny memorial ring true:

These are patriots' graves, friends of humble, honest toil, these were your peers. Fervent affection kindled these hearts, honest industry employed these hands.

ENDNOTES

Part I: Catastrophe at the Allegheny Arsenal, September 17, 1862

1. Fleming, George T., "Arsenal Blowup Recalled by Big Blast—Eddystone Disaster Rivaled by Holocaust Here—September 17, 1862," *The Pittsburgh Gazette Times*, April 22, 1917, p. 2.
2. Letter from Colonel John Symington to General James W. Ripley, Allegheny Arsenal Records, National Archives, Philadelphia, PA, October 2, 1861.
3. "The Arsenal Catastrophe: Coroner's Investigation," *The Pittsburgh Daily Post*, September 20, 1862, p. 3.
4. "The Arsenal Catastrophe: Coroner's Investigation," *Pittsburgh Post*, September 20, 1862, p. 3.
5. As quoted in "Allegheny Arsenal Explosion: Pittsburgh's Worst Day during the Civil War" by Marylynne Pitz, *Pittsburgh Post-Gazette*, September 16, 2012.
    http://www.post-gazette.com/life/lifestyle/2012/09/16/Allegheny-Arsenal-Explosion-Pittsburgh-s-worst-day-during-the-Civil-War/stories/201209160145
6. "Appalling Disaster! Explosion at the U.S. Arsenal," *Pittsburgh Gazette*, September 18, 1862, p. 3.
7. "A Painful Rumor," *Pittsburgh Gazette*, September 19, 1862, p. 3.
8. http://www.nps.gov/anti/learn/historyculture/casualties.htm
9. "Appalling Disaster! Explosion at the U.S. Arsenal, Extent of the Damage," *Pittsburgh Gazette*, September 18, 1862, p. 3.

Part II: A Horrible Accident at the Confederate States Laboratory, March 13, 1863

1. "Local Matters: Government Works," *Richmond Dispatch*, January 2, 1863, p. 1.
2. *Richmond Examiner*, March 14, 1863, as transcribed on http://www.mdgorman.com/Written_Accounts/ Examiner/1863/richmond_examiner_31463a.htm
3. David L. Burton, "Friday the 13th: Richmond's Great Home Front Disaster," *Civil War Times Illustrated*, Vol. 21, No. 6, October 1982, p. 38.
4. Ibid.
5. Ibid., p. 39.
6. Katherine Calos, "Brown's Island Munitions Explosion Was Worst Wartime Disaster in Richmond," *Richmond Times-Dispatch*, March 4, 2013. http://www.richmond.com/news/ local/city-of-richmond/article_9683aac6-847f-11e2-b033-0019bb30f31a.html)
7. Ibid.
8. *Richmond Examiner*, April 4, 1863, as transcribed on http://www.mdgorman.com/Written_Accounts/ Examiner/1863/richmond_examiner_4463a.htm

Part III: Stars and Fire at the Washington Arsenal, June 17, 1864

1. "Terrible Calamity at the Washington Arsenal," *Daily National Intelligencer*, June 18, 1864, np.
2. "The Episode Yesterday at the Arsenal," *[Washington] Evening Star*, June 18, 1864, p. 1.
3. Brian Bergin, *The Washington Arsenal Explosion: Civil War Disaster in the Capital*, Charleston, SC: The History Press, p. 56.
4. Ibid., p. 57.
5. Ibid., p. 59.
6. "The Episode Yesterday at the Arsenal," p. 1.
7. Ibid.
8. Ibid.
9. "Further of the Explosions," *[Washington] Evening Star*, June 18, 1864, second edition, p. 2.
10. "The Funeral of the Victims of the Arsenal Explosion," *[Washington] Evening Star*, June 20, 1864, p. 1.
11. Joshua Wolf Shenk, *Lincoln's Melancholy: How Depression Challenged a President and Fueled His Greatness*, Boston: Mariner Books/Houghton Mifflin Company, 2005, p. 203.

SELECTED BIBLIOGRAPHY

Books

Alexander, General E. P., Chief of Artillery, Longstreet's Corps. *The American Civil War: A Critical Narrative*. London: Siegle, Hill, and Co, 1908.

Bergin, Brian. *The Washington Arsenal Explosion*. Charleston, SC: History Press, 2012.

Frank, Lisa Tendrich, editor. "Economy and Work: Munitions Factories." *The World of the Civil War: A Daily Life Encyclopedia*. Santa Barbara, California: Greenwood, An imprint of ABC-CLIO, LLC, 2015.

_____. "Bread Riots." *Women in the American Civil War*. Volume I: A–G. Santa Barbara, California: Greenwood, An imprint of ABC-CLIO, LLC, 2008, pp. 140–141.

_____. "Government Girls." *Women in the American Civil War*. Volume I: A–G. Santa Barbara, California: Greenwood, An imprint of ABC-CLIO, LLC, 2008, pp. 140–141.

_____. "Immigrant Women." *Women in the American Civil War*. Volume II: H–Z. Santa Barbara, California: Greenwood, An imprint of ABC-CLIO, LLC, 2008.

_____. "Wartime Employment." *Women in the American Civil War*. Volume I: A–G. Santa Barbara, California: Greenwood, An imprint of ABC-CLIO, LLC, 2008, pp. 80–86.

Giesberg, Judith. *Army at Home: Women and the Civil War on the Northern Home Front*. Chapel Hill, North Carolina: University of North Carolina Press, 2009.

Marten, James. *The Children's Civil War*. Chapel Hill, North Carolina: The University of North Carolina Press, 1998.

Massey, Mary Elizabeth. *Women in the Civil War*. Lincoln, Nebraska: University of Nebraska Press, 1966.

Miller, Francis Trevelyan and Robert Sampson Lanier. "The Ordnance of the Confederacy." In *Photographic History of the Civil War in Ten Volumes: Volume 5, Forts and Artillery*, edited by O. E. Hunt. Springfield, Massachusetts: Patriot Publishing Company, 1911.

Shenk, Joshua Wolf. *Lincoln's Melancholy: How Depression Challenged a President and Fueled His Greatness*. Boston: Mariner Books/Houghton Mifflin Company, 2005.

Silber, Nina. *Daughters of the Union: Northern Women Fight the Civil War*. Cambridge, Massachusetts: Harvard University Press, 2005.

Thomas, Dean S. *Roundball to Rimfire: A History of Civil War Small Arms Ammunition: Part One*. Gettysburg, VA: Thomas Publications, 1997.

United States Army Ordinance Department. *The Ordinance Manual for the Use of the Officers of the United States Army*. Third Edition. Philadelphia, PA: J. B. Lippincott & Co., 1862.

Newspapers (Primary Source Articles)

"Allegheny Arsenal Disaster—Continuance of the Investigation, The." *The Pittsburgh Gazette*. Pittsburgh, Pennsylvania, September 23, 1862. https://www.newspapers.com/image/?spot=3235657.

"Allegheny Arsenal Explosion." *The Pittsburgh Gazette*. Pittsburgh, Pennsylvania, November 11, 1862. https://www.newspapers.com/image/?spot=3236343.

"Appalling Disaster! Explosion at the U.S. Arsenal." *The Pittsburgh Gazette*. Pittsburgh, Pennsylvania, September 18, 1862. https://www.newspapers.com/image/?spot=4095526.

"Arsenal Catastrophe: Coroner's Investigation, The." *The Pittsburgh Daily Post*, September 20, 1862. https://www.newspapers.com/image/?spot=4087506.

"Arsenal Catastrophe, The. Obsequies of the Victims." Local News. *National Republican*. Washington, D.C., June 20, 1864. https://www.newspapers.com/image/?spot=4407225.

"Arsenal Disaster, The. Conclusion of the Testimony. No Verdict Yet." *The Pittsburgh Gazette*. Pittsburgh, Pennsylvania, September 25, 1862. https://www.newspapers.com/image/?spot=3236354.

"Arsenal Disaster, The. Public Meeting and Prompt Action of Citizens." *The Pittsburgh Daily Post*, September 19, 1862. https://www.newspapers.com/image/?spot=3236282.

"Benevolent Work Begun, The." *National Republican*. Washington, D.C., June 22, 1864. https://www.newspapers.com/image/?spot=5160697.

"Catastrophe at the Arsenal. The Coroner's Inquest. Identification of Bodies. Burial of the Dead." *The Pittsburgh Daily Post*, September 19, 1862. https://www.newspapers.com/image/?spot=4087506.

"Coroner's Jury and the Arsenal Explosion, The." *The Pittsburgh Gazette*. Pittsburgh, Pennsylvania, September 30, 1862. https://www.newspapers.com/image/?spot=3236381.

"Coroner's Jury on the Arsenal Catastrophe, The. The Verdict: Two Jurors Dissent." *The Pittsburgh Daily Post*, September 29, 1862. https://www.newspapers.com/image/?spot=4257939.

"Explosion at the Arsenal, The. Testimony Before the Coroner's Jury. Accurate List of the Killed." *The Pittsburgh Gazette*. Pittsburgh, Pennsylvania, September 20, 1862. https://www.newspapers.com/image/?spot=4267917.

"Explosion Yesterday at the Arsenal, The." *Evening Star*. Washington, D.C., June 18, 1864, p. 1. https://www.newspapers.com/image/?spot=4979424.

"Funeral of the Victims of the Arsenal Explosion, The. Affecting Scenes—Interesting Obsequies, etc." *Evening Star*. Washington, D.C., June 20, 1864, p. 1. https://www.newspapers.com/image/?spot=5160853.

"Government Works." *Daily Dispatch*. Richmond, Virginia, January 2, 1863. https://www.newspapers.com/image/?spot=4970058.

"Late Explosion at the Arsenal—Verdict of the Coroner's Jury, The." *The Pittsburgh Gazette*. Pittsburgh, Pennsylvania, September 18, 1862. https://www.newspapers.com/image/?spot=3235633.

"News of the Explosion." *Chester Times*. April 10, 1917. https://www.newspapers.com/image/5387162/

"Painful Rumor, A." *The Pittsburgh Gazette*. Pittsburgh, Pennsylvania, September 19, 1862. https://www.newspapers.com/image/?spot=4952682.

Richmond Examiner articles archived at
http:///www.mdgorman.com.
"Explosion at C.S. Laboratory." March 14, 1863.
"Buildings of the C.S. Laboratory Have Been Rebuilt."
April 4, 1863.
"Terrible Laboratory Explosion on Brown's Island—
Between Forty and Fifty Persons Killed and Wounded—
Horrible Scenes." March 14, 1863.

Richmond Sentinel articles archived at
http:///www.mdgorman.com.
"Another Victim." March 20, 1863.
"Another Victim." March 21, 1863.
"Benefit for the Laboratory Sufferers." March 26, 1863.
"Body Found." April 13, 1863.

"Died of Her Injuries." March 18, 1863.

"Disaster at the Laboratory—List of Killed and Wounded, The." March 16, 1863.

Richmond Dispatch articles archived at http:///www.mdgorman. com.

"Confederate States Laboratory Department, The." January 5, 1863.

"Terrible Explosion." January 28, 1862.

Richmond Enquirer articles archived at http:///www.mdgorman.com.

"Confederate States Laboratory, The." January 6, 1863.

"Terrible Explosion—Between Forty and Fifty Females Killed and Wounded." March 14, 1863.

Richmond Whig articles archived at http:///www.mdgorman. com.

"Cartridge Factory, The." July 9, 1861.

"Panic at the Cartridge Factory." September 27, 1861.

"Sad Result, A." *National Republican*. Washington, D.C., June 21, 1864. https://www.newspapers.com/image/?spot=4407249.

"Washington Arsenal Explosion, The." *The Pittsburgh Gazette*. Pittsburgh, Pennsylvania, June 22, 1864. https://www.newspapers.com/image/?spot=3235454.

"Terrible Calamity at the Washington Arsenal." *Daily National Intelligencer*. Washington, D.C., June 18, 1864. http://www.mcelfresh.ws/DC_arsenalfire.html.

Contemporary Magazine and Newspaper Articles

Burton, David L. "Friday the 13th: Richmond's Great Homefront Disaster." *Civil War Times Illustrated*. Volume 21. No. 6, October 1982, pp. 36–41.

Calos, Katherine. "Brown's Island Munitions Explosion Was Worst Wartime Disaster in Richmond." *Richmond Times-Dispatch*. March 4, 2013.

Connor, Michael. "The Next Page: The Allegheny Arsenal Explosion—Pittsburgh's Civil War Carnage." *Pittsburgh Post-Gazette*. September 12, 2010.

Pitz, Marylynne. "Allegheny Arsenal Explosion: Pittsburgh's Worst Day During the Civil War." *Pittsburgh Post-Gazette*. September 16, 2012.

Rubis, Karl. "Tragedy on the Homefront: Industrial Accidents at Ordnance Arsenals during the Civil War." *Ordnance Magazine*. Spring 2015, pp. 12-14.

Online Articles and Blogs

Ballman, Robert E. And John Joseph Wallis, eds. *American Economic Growth and Standards of Living Before the Civil War*. Chicago: University of Chicago Press, 1992, page 48. http://www.nber.org/books/gall92-1. Accessed December 15, 2015.

"Emergence of 'Women's Sphere,' The." Article 25e at USHistory. org. http://www.ushistory.org/us/25e.asp.

"Friction Primers: How They Were Made and How to Make Them Today." http://www.gunneyg.info/html/friction%20primers. htm.

Geisberg, Judith. "Explosion at the Allegheny Arsenal." http://www.historynet.com/explosion-at-the-allegheny-arsenal.htm.

History.com Staff. "Child Labor." http://www.history.com/topics/child-labor, 2009.

MacLean, Maggie. "Allegheny Arsenal Explosion." Civil War Women blog. http://www.civilwarwomenblog.com/allegheny-arsenal-explosion.htm

_____. "Women and Girls in the Brown's Island Explosion." Civil War Women blog. http://www.civilwarwomenblog.com/women-and-girls-in-the-browns-island-explosion.htm

O'Neill, Robert. "The Mystery Lives Where 139 Perished." *Philadelphia Inquirer*. April 19, 1992. http://articles.philly.com/1992-04-19/news/26001794_1_shells-munitions-plant-sabotage

Powers, Tom and James Wudarczuk. "Behind the Scenes of the Allegheny Arsenal Explosion." *Pennsylvania Legacies* 13 (1-2). The Historical Society of Pennsylvania, 2013, pp. 42–55. doi:10.5215/pennlega.13.1-2.0042.

Rafferty, Colleen. "The Allegheny Arsenal Explosion of 1862." *History Matters*. Volume 23. Issue 10. National Council of History Education. June 2011. pp. 6–9. http://www.nche.net/document.doc?id=4.

Rubis, Karl. "The History of Ordnance in America." U.S. Army Ordnance Corps and School. www.goordnance.army.mil/history/ORDhistory.html. Accessed January 20, 2016.

Spinnenweber, Lawrence J. Jr. "Pittsburgh's Bloodiest Day." http://www.civilwarinteractive.come/ArticlePittsburgh-BloodyDay.htm

Archives and Census Records

Ancestry.com. *1850 United States Federal Census* [database online]. Provo, Utah: Ancestry.com Operations, Inc., 2009. Accessed March 30, 2016. Various names of victims and/or family members.

Ancestry.com. *1860 United States Federal Census* [database online]. Provo, Utah: Ancestry.com Operations, Inc., 2009. Accessed March 30, 2016. Various names of victims and/or family members.

"Arsenal Payroll Records—1862." National Archives. Mid-Atlantic Region. Expenditures, Statements, Payrolls, Allegheny Arsenal, RG156. http://www.archives.gov/philadelphia/exhibits/allegheny-arsenal/arsenal-payroll.html.

"Harper's Weekly—Image of a Munitions Factory." Library of Congress. Washington, D.C. http://www.archives.gov/philadelphia/exhibits/allegheny-arsenal/harpers-weekly.html.

"Layout of the Allegheny Arsenal Grounds." Library of Congress. Washington, D.C. http://www.archives.gov/philadelphia/exhibits/allegheny-arsenal/layout-of-grounds.html.

"Letter from Colonel John Symington to General James W. Ripley." Allegheny Arsenal Records. National Archives. Philadelphia, Pennsylvania, October 2, 1861.

"Pittsburgh Arsenal Explosion." House Report, June 19, 1882. http://www.archives.gov/philadelphia/exhibits/allegheny-arsenal/house-report.html.

RECOMMENDED READING

Civil War (Nonfiction)

Abbott, Karen. *Liar, Temptress, Soldier, Spy: Four Women Undercover in the Civil War*. Harper, 2014.

Anderson, Tanya. *Tillie Pierce: Teen Eyewitness to the Battle of Gettysburg*. Quindaro Press, 2016.

Catton, Bruce. *The Civil War* (American Heritage Books). Mariner Books, 2014.

Civil War: A Visual History, The. Dorling Kindersley (Smithsonian), 2011.

Cordell, M. R. *Courageous Women of the Civil War: Soldiers, Spies, Medics, and More* (Women of Action series). Chicago Review Press, 2016.

Eickhoff, Diane. *Clarina Nichols: Frontier Crusader for Women's Rights*. Quindaro Press, 2016.

Freedman, Russell. *A Savage Thunder: Antietam and the Bloody Road to Freedom*. Margaret K. McElderry Books, 2009.

Hyslop, Steve. *Eyewitness to the Civil War*. National Geographic, 2006.

Martin, Iain C. *Gettysburg: The True Account of Two Young Heroes in the Greatest Battle of the Civil War*. Sky Pony Press, 2013.

McPherson, James M. *Battle Cry of Freedom: The Civil War Era*. Oxford University Press, 1988.

Moss, Marissa. *A Soldier's Secret: The Incredible True Story of Sarah Edmonds: a Civil War Hero*. Amulet Books, 2012.

Murphy, Jim. *The Boys' War: Confederate and Union Soldiers Talk About the Civil War*. Houghton Mifflin Harcourt Books for Young Readers, 1990.

Silvey, Anita. *I'll Pass for Your Comrade: Women Soldiers in the Civil War*. Clarion Books, 2009.

Warren, Andrea. *Under Siege!: Three Children at the Civil War Battle for Vicksburg*. Farrar Straus and Giroux, 2009.

Werner, Emmy E. *Reluctant Witnesses: Children's Voices from the Civil War*. Westview Press, 1998.

Women and Child Labor Reform (Nonfiction)

Bartoletti, Susan Campbell. *Growing Up in Coal Country*. HMH Books for Young Readers, 1999.

Bartoletti, Susan Campbell. *Kids on Strike!* Sandpiper Books, 2003.

Burgan, Michael. *Breaker Boys: How a Photograph Helped End Child Labor*. Compass Point, 2011.

Colman, Penny. *Rosie the Riveter: Women Working on the Home Front in World War II*. Crown Books for Young Readers, 1998.

Colman, Penny. *Strike! The Bitter Struggle of American Workers from Colonial Times to the Present*. Millbrook Press, 1995.

Colman, Penny. *A Woman Unafraid: The Achievements of Frances Perkins*. iUniverse, 2010.

Currie, Stephen. *We Have Marched Together: The Working Children's Crusade*. Lerner Publishing Group, 1997.

Dash, J. *We Shall Not Be Moved: The Women's Factory Strike of 1909*. Scholastic, 1996.

Freedman, Russell. *Kids at Work: Lewis Hine and the Crusade Against Child Labor*. HMH Books for Young Readers, 1998.

Kraft, Betsy. *Mother Jones: One Woman's Fight for Labor*. Clarion, 1995.

Marrin, Albert. *Flesh & Blood So Cheap: The Triangle Fire and Its Legacy*. Knopf, 2011.

Mullenbach, Cheryl. *Double Victory: How African American Women Broke Race and Gender Barriers to Help Win World War II*. Chicago Review Press, 2013.

Pasachoff, Naomi. *Frances Perkins: Champion of the New Deal*. Oxford University Press, 2000.

Stanley, Jerry. *Big Annie of Calumet: A True Story of the Industrial Revolution*. Crown Publishers, 1996.

PHOTO AND ILLUSTRATION CREDITS

Page 25: Illustration by Cary Robert Dean.

Page 27: Illustration by Cary Robert Dean based on a design by Tom Powers, Power Media and Design.

Page 27 (photo): Missouri History Museum.

Page 31: Michael Simens and www.HistoricalArms.com.

Page 37: National Archives and Records Administration.

Pages 45, 68, and 106: Eric Anderson.

Page 76: Mike Bordonie.

Pages 91, 121: Library of Congress.

Page 99: National Defense University Libraries.

INDEX

ABOUT THE AUTHOR

TANYA ANDERSON IS AN AWARD-WINNING AUTHOR AND EDITOR OF BOOKS FOR YOUNG READERS. She has worked for more than twenty years in various editorial functions for Pages Publishing Group, *Guideposts for Teens*, SRA/McGraw-Hill, Darby Creek Publishing, and School Street Media, her own business.

Anderson is the author of more than thirty books published in children's and educational book markets. Her book, *Tillie Pierce: Teen Eyewitness to the Battle of Gettysburg*, is also a narrative nonfiction book for young readers. It was a Junior Library Guild Selection and won the 2014 IBPA Benjamin Franklin Award for Teen Nonfiction. *Gunpowder Girls: The True Stories of Three Civil War Tragedies* is a Junior Library Guild Selection for 2016–2017.

Anderson lives in Springfield, Ohio, most of the year, but retreats to Palm Harbor, Florida, when it gets too cold. Her website is www.tanyaandersonbooks.com. She has also created a website to share even more information about this topic at www.gunpowdergirlsbook.com.